CONSTRAINT
BY
COPYRIGHT

CONSTRAINT

BY

COPYRIGHT

A Report on "Official" and "Private" Practices

By M. B. SCHNAPPER

Public Affairs Press, Washington, D. C.

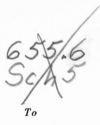

To

STANLEY B. FROSH

BERNARD S. WHITE

HARRY N. ROSENFIELD

Attorneys For the Public

Copyright, 1960, by Public Affairs Press
419 New Jersey Avenue, S.E., Washington 3, D. C.
Printed in the United States of America
Library of Congress Catalog Card No. 60-53619

PREFACE

Whatever the shortcomings of this work, they are substantially due to lack of time and resources with which to do research in depth. But while unlimited time and resources would undoubtedly have made the author's task easier, it is doubtful that these advantages would have been sufficient to surmount the obstacles that inevitably arise when a person tries to get at facts regarding questionable activities of governmental officials. Almost everywhere he turns his inquiries are greeted—or, rather, blocked— by oblique faces, polite evasion, double-talk, equivocation, stony silence, and, in some cases, outright misrepresentation. Even through judicial proceedings getting at the facts is a frustrating and discouraging experience.

No private individual, no matter how resourceful, can possibly get at all the facts concerning the nature and extent of abuse of copyrighting by and through public officials. That is or should be a responsibility of government itself. In view of the fact that revision of the Copyright Act is high on the agenda of the 87th Congress it is both timely and fitting that that body undertake investigation of the problem under the terms of Senate Resolution 240[1] authorizing the Senate Subcommittee on Patents, Trademarks, and Copyrights to make studies enabling Congress to determine what statutory changes are necessary.

The problems set forth in these pages are in large part due to loopholes in the Copyright Act. The present phrasing of Section 8 is far too loose; when it was formulated in 1909 copyrighting by public officials was not a problem of consequence because the opportunities worth risks were negligible.[2] Fifty years ago, for example, private enterprise, not government, was the nation's chief source of economic and scientific information. Today almost exactly the opposite is true and it is no mere coincidence that there appears to be a close correlation between the marked increase of copyrighting by public officials, whether misguided or honorably intentioned, and the rising pecuniary value of the information covered by such copyrighting.

It need hardly be pointed out that Public Affairs Press, like all publishers of the printed word, has a vested interest in copyright as a valuable property right. Superficially it would seem folly for the Press to question

[1] 86th Congress, Second Session.

[2] Significantly, it was devised to prevent exactly what has occurred in recent years. See pp. 98-102 for details regarding why the Copyright Act was amended by a provision expressly prohibiting copyrights on official material.

the use of a device indispensable from a profit-making viewpoint, particularly in the case of a Washington publishing house that best can feather its nest by currying favor with government officials. Nevertheless, from the viewpoint of the public and, in the long run, of publishers of every type, unbridled copyrighting of official material is dangerous. It is subversive in its effect upon the Constitutional rights of the American people and the rights of a free press in a democratic society. Today, it is true, a newspaper, magazine or book publisher stands to gain temporary advantage by securing exclusive rights to material made available by an official, but tomorrow every publisher has much to lose if governmental copyrighting becomes a general practice.

As a publisher of more than 1500 works, written chiefly by scholars, in such fields as political science, economics, sociology, history, military affairs, etc.—fields in which government sources of information are of prime importance—Public Affairs Press cannot help but be keenly conscious of the unfortunate effects of improper copyrighting by public officials. Such copyrighting is invariably preceded by withholding and seemingly inexplicable disappearance of source materials indispensable to scholars. For obvious reasons a public official who plans to publish and copyright material over which he wields control or can influence control through others in the public service has strong reasons for using those controls to his advantage.[3] He is hardly likely to go out of his way in order to let this material become accessible to "outsiders" or even possible competitors within his own agency or other government departments. Moreover, if he is familiar with the withholding requisites of the Copyright Act (see page 29 for details) he has no choice but to withhold from others that which he plans to copyright; should he allow his material to become available to the public prior to copyright registration he thereby endangers the validity of his registration.

The author is, of course, solely to blame for the shortcomings of this work and the assertions made herein. Such merit as it may have is very much attributable to the wise and unselfish counsel the author derived from his providential and enriching friendship with Stanley B. Frosh, Bernard S. White, and Harry N. Rosenfield. Without the unstinted support and advice of these three public-spirited attorneys the battle against improper copyrighting would have been lost before it began.

Others to whom the author is deeply indebted are Walter B. Wheeler, E. William Marclay, and Clarence M. Burton, loyal and conscientious colleagues; Belle Martin and Robert Burt who greatly facilitated preparation and publication of this work.

[3] For details of how this has operated to the disadvantage of newspapers see page 36.

Among those who have been helpful in very special ways are V. M. Newton, Jr., President of Sigma Delta Chi and Chairman of its Freedom of Information Committee; Clark Mollenhoff, Washington correspondent of the Des Moines Register-Tribune; H. M. Somers, Chairman of the Political Science Department at Haverford College; Herbert Brucker, editor of the Hartford Courant; E. Wilder Spaulding, former chief of the State Department's publication program; B. W. Huebsch, editor of Viking Press, and Sylvan Gotshal, emiment member of the New York Bar.

M. B. SCHNAPPER

Editor, Public Affairs Press
Washington, D. C.

CONTENTS

1

FOREVIEW

Subconsciously the author began to write this book back in 1933 when he laid the groundwork for Public Affairs Press as a publishing house "designed to promote the spread of authoritative facts and significant opinions concerning contemporary social and economic problems." Since the nation's capital was rapidly becoming a major source for such facts and opinions, Washington seemed exactly the right place for the Press to establish its headquarters. As soon became evident, a practical and useful service could be performed by making more readily available to the public governmental information on vital issues of the day. This service was especially gratifying in that it evoked considerable commendation by government officials, educators, and the public at large.[1] If this phase of the publishing activities of the Press was not commercially feasible by normal standards this was adequately made up for by the prestige involved and the earnings accruing from other publishing ventures of the Press.[2]

Gradually, almost imperceptibly until the end of the war, things began to change in the national capital as the Press expanded into the reference book field. Less and less government information was accessible while more and more of it began turning up under the copyrights of officials who devised ingenious ways and means of transforming public property into private property. The situation was strange but it definitely was not alarming. Where was the harm if now and then a public servant earned a few extra dollars this way? Little by little, however, the situation changed markedly. Transforming public property into private property became a sizeable extra-curricular activity: great masses of information began disappearing from official files and reappearing under the private copyrights of the very persons who had commissioned preparation of this material for the federal government.

What became inconspicuously, but unconcealably, apparent was the ex-

---

[1] See exhibits on pages 37 and 38 regarding Army pamphlets removed from copyright restrictions at insistence of the author in May 1945. Among those who expressed specific appreciation of the public service rendered by Public Affairs Press in reprinting governmental matter were Supreme Court Justice Frank Murphy, Attorney General Tom Clark, Secretary of the Navy Frank Knox, and Secretary of War Henry L. Stimson.

[2] See pages 94 and 96.

tensiveness of copyrighting in fields where the federal government was opening up new horizons at great expense to the nation—in atomic energy, in electronics, in astronautics, etc. Also noticeable but none too conspicuously, was the fact that exclusive publishing rights were being sold to several giant firms in a position to pay generously for the privilege of monopoly control over government information. If these circumstances didn't make much sense from the public's viewpoint, they at least made some sense for the contracting parties. What made almost no sense was the epidemic of copyright notices that began to pockmark official documents printed by the Government Printing Office and sold by the Superintendent of Documents.[3]

What made the least sense was what happened in October 1958 when Admiral H. G. Rickover, a public servant who deserves well of his country but who nonetheless owes much to that country, bluntly informed Public Affairs Press it could not quote so much as a sentence from speeches he had prepared, processed, and disseminated as official press releases of the Defense Department and the Atomic Energy Commission. Why not? They were, averred the Admiral with more heat than light, his personal property despite all their official characteristics. Here, then, was the outer limit, the *reductio ad absurdum*, of a preposterous and yet dangerous trend. Here was a challenge which could not be ignored. It has not been.

[3] When in 1945 the author first challenged copyrights on documents printed by the Government Printing Office, the Register of Copyright, Sam B. Warner, responded matter of factly: "While Section 7 [now Section 8] of the Copyright Act prohibits copyright on government publications, it does not define what constitutes such publications." (Letter dated March 17, 1945).

Blood Concentrations Following Oral Administration of Chlortetracycline Hydrochloride and Chlortetracycline Base, With and Without Sodium Hexametaphosphate

HENRY WELCH, WILLIAM W. WRIGHT, AND C. N. LEWIS

Department of Health, Education, and Welfare, Food and Drug Administration, Washington, D. C.

PREVIOUS studies in these laboratories[1,2] have shown that both the phosphate complex of tetracycline and a mixture of tetracycline base and sodium hexametaphosphate produced markedly higher blood concentrations in man than tetracycline hydrochloride or tetracycline base alone. In the present investigation a four-way crossover study has been made using chlortetracycline base and chlortetracycline hydrochloride,* both with and without sodium hexametaphosphate (380 mg. per capsule).

EXPERIMENTAL

All four preparations were in capsule form and filled to contain 250 mg. of chlortetracycline hydrochloride activity. All preparations were tested in the same individuals. The 20 volunteer subjects were healthy adult men, predominantly Negro, doing light physical labor. They were maintained on a uniform diet and a rigid time schedule. At least three days were allowed between the days on which medications were given. That this was sufficient is evidenced by the fact that control blood samples taken just prior to the administration of each drug were negative for chlortetracycline activity in all cases. Each subject was given one capsule of drug followed by two ounces of water and watched to see that it was swallowed. The drugs were administered four to four and one-half hours after breakfast, which time was one-half to one hour before lunch. Blood specimens were secured immediately before and at two, three, and six hours after medication. All specimens were numbered as the only means of identification and returned promptly to the laboratory for assay. The blood samples were centrifuged and the serum removed. However, while the two and three hour specimens were assayed on the day they were obtained, the control and six hour serum samples were frozen and assayed the following day. The concentrations of chlortetracycline were determined by the cylinder-plate assay technique using *Bacillus cereus* var. *mycoides* as the assay organism.[3] Chlortetracycline hydrochloride was used as the standard of comparison.

RESULTS

The individual serum concentrations (μg./ml.) found at two, three, and six

---

* The trade name of Lederle Laboratories Division, American Cyanamid Co., for chlortetracycline is Aureomycin.

Received for Publication: May 21, 1957

Reprinted from ANTIBIOTIC MEDICINE & CLINICAL THERAPY, *Vol. IV No. 7,* July, 1957
© Copyright 1957 by MD Publications, Inc. All rights reserved.

Copyrighting of material such as the above helped add $287,000 to the personal income of Dr. Welch, Director of the Antibiotics Division of the Food and Drug Administration. Details of his copyrighting activities are set forth in hearings held by Senate Subcommittee on Anti-Trust and Monopoly in May and June of 1960.

Dr. Henry Welch
Earnings derived from the operations of
Medical Encyclopedia, Inc.
1953 to March 31, 1960 (Note)

Earnings distributed to Dr. Welch in
the form of salary payments:

1954	$ 5,000.00
1955	1,500.00
1956	1,500.00
1957	10,000.00
1958	none
1959	11,250.00
1960, through March	7,500.00

Total earnings distributed as salary $ 36,750.00

Residual earning retained in the corporation:

Net worth, February 28, 1959 $52,751.41 (1)

One half of the net worth belonging to
Dr. and Mrs. Welch's one-half interest $ 26,375.70
in the corporation

Total earnings, distributed as salary or
residual to the credit of Dr. Welch $ 63,125.70

M. D. Publications
Computations of Payments to Dr. Welch
1953 through 1959

	Sale of Advertising	Sale of Reprints	Charges for Extra Pages	Payments to Dr. Welch
Net Advertising	$265,581			
Payments to Dr. Welch, at 7½%	$ 20,294.43			$ 20,294.43
Total Sales of Reprints		$685,760		
Less costs and overhead		339,164		
Net Profit		346,596		
Payments to Dr. Welch at 50%		$173,293.02		173,293.02
Total charged for Extra pages			$ 69,454	
Less costs and overhead			30,547	
Net Profit			$ 38,907	
Payments to Dr. Welch at 25%			$ 9,726.91	9,726.91
Settlement on British Edition				18,972.89
Commission on Bulk Sales				1,729.45
Total payments to Dr. Welch				$224,016.70

Extracts from Senate documents providing a breakdown of the
$287,000 Dr. Welch received through extra-curricula publishing
activities facilitated by official resources available to him as a top
echelon officer of the U. S. Food and Drug Administration.

2

PRIVATE VERSUS PUBLIC

The purpose of this report is to call to the attention of the American people a problem vitally affecting the interests of every citizen: extensive copyrighting of official material[1] by public officials who flagrantly disregard or deftly by-pass laws barring such activities.

By resort to monopoly via copyrighting government officers are placing private property restrictions on and around a vast amount of official information that has cost the taxpayer countless billions of dollars. These restrictions are restrictions upon every citizen of this and every other nation for a minimum of 28 years and a maximum of 56 years.

Inherent in copyrighting by public officials is presumption of the right to suppress completely whatever they consider their personal property and arrogation of private authority to restrict access to or use of such property if and when they should see fit to disclose its nature.[2]

It is submitted that, subject to fully warranted exceptions, copyrighting of material of a predominantly official nature by or through government officers is contrary to (1) the free speech and free press guarantees of the Bill of Rights, (2) the Constitutional oath every public official is required to take, (3) the provisions of the Constitution sanctioning copyrighting under limited circumstances, and (4) the very specific prohibitions of the Copyright Act.

Copyrighting by government officers of official material is equivalent to government by private copyright. Officials are the living embodiment of government; if this were not the case there would be no government.

---

[1] Official material, the author contends, is material which for all practical (and substantive) purposes could not exist without the benefit of official knowledge, official resources (including official funds), official facilities, and official auspices. Existence of only one of these factors is pertinent but not decisive; existence of several factors simultaneously appears to approximate evidence of official status.

Articles, speeches, books written by government workers under circumstances which are substantially private—particularly in the case of persons whose duties are subject to supervisory scrutiny and in the case of works that do not conflict with the duties of the author—are not considered official.

[2] As Philip Wittenberg, one of the nation's leading copyright experts, has pointed out, "the dominion over the work lies with the author [or copyright claimant]. He may determine when, where, and to whom it shall be divulged and by what means of communication it is to be conveyed." The Law of Literary Property, 1957, p. 60.

CONSTRAINT BY COPYRIGHT

An official who copyrights material of a preponderantly official nature is in effect creating government by private copyright.

Government by private copyright is indefensible. It makes no more sense than government by private individuals for private purposes.

It cannot be too strongly emphasized that abuse by upper echelon officials of the privileges and resources available to them is the chief concern of this report. Such abuse is detrimental to the interests of government workers in general in that it may, if not checked, arouse public indignation to the point where no clear differentiation is made between what is reasonable and what is unreasonable, what is desirable and what is undesirable.

It is both reasonable and highly desirable that government workers be encouraged to contribute to the sum of human knowledge through newspapers, magazines, and books. The nation wants and needs the benefit of whatever they know. Far too many of the problems confronting modern society remain unsolved because not enough is known about their nature and their solution. And despite all the progress that America has made in the arts and sciences much remains to be achieved.

There is no reason in the world why government workers should not in their private capacities pass on to their fellow citizens what they know and what they think. If in the process of their efforts in this connection they should incidentally use government facilities this hardly matters from the public's viewpoint. What does matter from the public's viewpoint is that public servants should not abuse the privileges and resources available to them as public servants. What does matter from the public's viewpoint is that public servants should not engage in activities conflicting with the public interest. What does matter from the public's viewpoint is that a clear line must be drawn between what is public and what is private. No act by a public servant should be made simultaneously to appear both public and private for the sake of the latter. Public property should never be transformed into private property. The sworn obligation to uphold the guarantees of the Bill of Rights should never be violated for the sake of private gain. The prohibitions of the Copyright Act should never be eluded or disregarded for any purpose—private, charitable or official; the purpose of this Act, it should always be remembered, is to prevent government agencies and government officials from placing restrictions on or around information that rightfully belongs to the entire nation.

Motives will vary, of course. Some officials will resort to copyrighting for the sake of increasing their incomes. Some will perhaps be motivated by a desire to raise funds for their favorite charities. Some will want to further their ambitions—political, professional, or purely personal— by granting, with or without compensation, exclusive publishing rights to

Should these seals of the United States be used in connection with the publication and promotion of privately copyrighted material?

a newspaper or magazine that can spread their fame in the right places. And some are bound to follow in Admiral Rickover's footsteps by permitting news periodicals to use his material provided that they comply with copyright stipulations that permit separate sale of the same material for personal and, possibly, charitable purposes.

By and large, the present tendency, if not stopped, will be to let the public know less and less free of charge and more and more at as high price as the traffic will bear. Why not?

The public official eager for cash or publicity will probably consider the stakes high enough to warrant running the risk of possible criticism; he will, if need be, sell or grant his copyright privileges while "his" material is "hot". But officials with discretion and patience will generally do their copyrighting as unobtrusively as possible, with a view to building up a substantial nest egg to draw upon after leaving the government service. To them the future will truly belong.

The problem is serious because, as the facts herein show, a vast amount of officially commissioned information has been and is being transformed into private property. Practically all of this information is derived from research made possible by countless billions provided by the nation's taxpayers in recent years. If it is not surprising neither is it reassuring that official information regarding atomic energy, astronautics, and other important new fields has attracted an inordinate amount of copyrighting.

Governmental copyrighting is by no means a problem sharply delineated by blacks and whites. While it is true that the basic principles of the Copyright Act and the Bill of Rights are quite simple, the restrictive practices that have sprung up are relatively complex. Hence, one of the purposes of this report is to show the variations of copyrighting by and through public officials without implying that each example is questionable or improper. At least some of the copyrights cited in these pages are altogether justifiable; others are definitely border-line cases; many appear to be distinctly doubtful.

In fairness to all concerned—especially to the public at large—a thorough investigation into all the facts should be undertaken by Congress. It is long overdue. And it is very much in order at the present time because revision of the Copyright Act is on the agenda of the new Congress. Not since 1909 has the national legislature taken a close look at copyrighting problems and practices.[3]

[3] For discussions of the need for changes in the Copyright Act see "Reflections on the Law of Copyright", Zechariah Chafee, Jr., Columbia Law Review, July and September, 1945; "Revision of the Copyright Law", Benjamin Kaplan, Law Library Journal, February, 1959; and Copyright Law Revision Studies prepared by personnel and consultants of the Copyright Office for the Senate Subcommittee on Patents, Trademarks, and Copyrights, 1960.

How come public officials have been copyrighting extensively in recent years? [4] Only an impartial Congressional investigation can provide a fully satisfactory explanation, but the following factors are at least partially to blame:

Loopholes in the Copyright Act.
Indifference by governmental agencies when the situation works
    to their advantage.
Absence of consistent standards and policies.
Arrogance by some high public officials.
Irresponsibility by some low public officials.
Desire for personal aggrandizement.
Eagerness for personal publicity.
Confusion as to what is "personal" and what is "public".
Honest uncertainty and/or ignorance.

In some—perhaps many—instances copyrighting has been resorted to by high-minded public officials motivated by what at least they considered the best of intentions, but such intentions do not justify circumscribing the First Amendment and violating the Copyright Act.

The things that happen when public officials consider themselves free agents constitute some of the shabbiest incidents of American history. Almost every black splotch in the annals of our national government is a splotch left by a public official who felt that he could do as he chose. The scandals of the Grant and Harding administrations, to cite two unfortunate periods of rampant malfeasance in public office, were the outgrowth of free-wheeling by men who had little regard for public interest or public trust.

Supreme Court Justice Louis Brandeis knew whereof he spoke when he said: "Experience should teach us to be most on our guard to protect

---

[4] A clear distinction should be drawn between copyrighting by or through a government officer of the original texts of official matter as against copyrighting of reprints of such matter after it enters the public domain as a government publication.

The former type of copyrighting covers all of the original text and is restrictive upon the public in every way for 28 to 56 years.

The other type of copyrighting—the copyrighting of reprints of public domain matter—merely pertains to new copy (introduction, artistic designs, etc.) that has been privately added. The original text necessarily remains in the public domain; anyone can quote or reprint this text at any time whatsoever without by-your-leave from anyone. Such copyrighting by officials or anyone else is fully consistent with the law and the public interest unless the following type of notice is used: "No portion of this work can be reprinted in any way unless permission is granted. . . . " Notices of this sort in reprints of public domain material are unwarranted and in all probability legally unjustifiable. Moreover, since clear indication of reprinted and official matter is desirable this should perhaps be stipulated in the revision of the Copyright Act.

liberty when the government's purposes are beneficient. . . . The greatest dangers to liberty lurk in the insidious encroachment by men of zeal, well-meaning but without understanding." [5]

Sensing the same dangers Justice Brandeis had in mind, Clark R. Mollen-hoff, a distinguished Pulitzer Prize winning journalist who is also an attorney, stated before a Senate Committee investigation of restriction of governmental information: "We must be guided by this principle: 'never trust a good man to make secret decisions for you, if it would frighten you to lodge the same power in an evil man or a man who is on the other side of the political fence'." [6]

Regardless of the reasons, good or bad, it is an unfortunate fact that one public official after another, marching in seemingly endless procession to the Copyright Office, has put to personal use privileged resources of the federal government which rightly belong to the entire nation. Wittingly or unwittingly, they have used public property to create private property on an unprecedented scale.

If copyrighting is fully justified in some instances, it is difficult to differentiate their branches in the forest of abuse that today engulfs the Copyright Office. It is altogether possible, indeed likely, that some officials aren't cognizant that copyrighting necessarily operates to the disadvantage of the public. No doubt some public servants have been led astray by practices that have become so general that nothing question-able appeared to be involved. It is even possible that some officials have resorted to copyrighting for what they consider the best interests of the public. But it is certainly not beyond the realm of liklihood that crass personal profit has been a motivation on the part of at least some copyrighting officials. In adding $287,000 to his income through the sale of copyrighted matter of a predominantly official nature, Dr. Henry Welch, chief of the Antibiotics Division of the U. S. Food and Drug Administration until a Senate Committee caught up with him, differed from other public servants only in degree. Where he stands head and shoulders above all the rest is in boldness; while others reached for peanuts unobtrusively, he went for the big money openly—aided and abetted by innumerable copyrights on officially prepared speeches, articles, and books.

Those public servants who have been most busily engaged in copyright-ing have not been obscure clerks seeking literary recognition about affairs far removed from government. A good many seem to be unusually ambi-tious officials eager to line their pockets, impress the public, and attain

---

[5] Olmstead v. United States, 277 U.S. 438, 479 (1928).
[6] Hearings on S. 921, 85th Congress, 2nd Session, Part II, April 16, 1958, p. 615.

CODE OF ETHICS
FOR GOVERNMENT SERVICE

Any Person In Government Service Should:

Put loyalty to the highest moral principles and to country above loyalty to persons, party, or Government department.

Uphold the Constitution, laws, and legal regulations of the United States and all governments therein and never be a party to their evasion.

Give a full day's labor for a full day's pay; giving to the performance of his duties his earnest effort and best thought.

Seek to find and employ more efficient and economical ways of getting tasks accomplished.

Never discriminate unfairly by the dispensing of special favors or privileges to anyone, whether for remuneration or not; and never accept, for himself or his family, favors or benefits under circumstances which might be construed by reasonable persons as influencing the performance of his governmental duties.

Make no private promises of any kind binding upon the duties of office, since a Government employee has no private word which can be binding on public duty.

Engage in no business with the Government, either directly or indirectly, which is inconsistent with the conscientious performance of his governmental duties.

Never use any information coming to him confidentially in the performance of governmental duties as a means for making private profit.

Expose corruption wherever discovered.

Uphold these principles, ever conscious that public office is a public trust.

(This Code of Ethics was agreed to by the House of Representatives and the Senate as House Concurrent Resolution 175 in the Second Session of the 85th Congress. The Code applies to all Government Employees and Office Holders.)

Under what circumstances is copyrighting by a public official consistent with this Code of Ethics for Government Service? Note third to last stricture: "Never use any information coming to him confidentially in the performance of governmental duties as a means for making private profit."

greater power—simultaneously if at all possible. Most are active participants in the formulation and execution of policies and programs critically affecting the present and future welfare of the American people.

In much of what such officials do they necessarily enjoy a wide exercise of discretion, but it is implicit that their acts must always be consistent with their oath of office and the basic laws of the land. As Mr. Justice Felix Frankfurter has stated, "a public man is, as it were, public property." [7]

The American people have a right to know everything that in any way affects the trusts and responsibilities of its top officials. Admiral Rickover was fully conscious of this when he conceded in one of his privately copyrighted speeches that "as a government servant my work is at all times subject to public scrutiny." However, a government official's work is not "at all times subject to public scrutiny" if his private copyrights permit him to place restrictions on public knowledge of his work and enable him to suppress, if he chooses, writings (including memoranda of an official character) incorporating what he has learned in his official capacity.

In his sphere of official responsibility and competence, the Supreme Court held in the case of Callaghan v. Myers, a government officer of policy-making rank has no proprietary rights as against the public at large. [7a]

It is as wrong for a public official to sell exclusive rights to predominantly official material as it is wrong for public servants to accept vicuna coats, oriental rugs and food freezers for services rendered in behalf of private parties. [9] Both types of transactions are fundamentally of the same nature; both are improper and unethical. *Public service and public property cannot and should not be subject to quid pro quo deals of a private nature.*

Nor is the situation markedly different if a public official turns over to a private charity remuneration he has received through the sale of material of a predominantly official character. While it is laudable of him to make contributions to eleemosynary institutions it is by no means commendable of him to do so under circumstances that are not fully ethical and

[7] Beauharnais v. Illinois, 343 U.S. 250, 263, 96 LL ed. 919, 72 S Ct 725.

[7a] 128 US 617, 32 L ed. 547, 9, Sec. 177.

[8] If, as has been asserted, public officials may copyright and sell predominantly official material as long as preparation of such matter was not specifically required by their official duties then it could be persuasively contended that Sherman Adams did nothing improper in accepting gifts from Bernard Goldfine for services his White House duties did not require him to perform. The same could be said in exculpation of practically every public official who has been forced to resign and clapped in prison because of extra-curricular activities not required by his duties. For a recent list of such officials see "Gleam Wears Off on Hound's Tooth", Washington Post, March 18, 1960.

possibly are illegal. *Giving charities money wrongfully acquired doesn't make wrong things right; it merely puts a better face on things.*[9]

Is the situation markedly different if a government agency or public official bestows upon a non-profit institution exclusive rights to publish and sell material of a predominantly official nature? Is this an extenuating circumstance that makes everything prim and proper? Hardly. There's nothing in the federal statutes that says a public official can assume common law copyright privileges over official material in order to make special benefits available to the most praiseworthy of non-profit organizations.[10]

Extenuating circumstances are not hard to come by for anyone in need of them. In justification of the extensive copyrighting activities that helped add \$287,000 to the income of Dr. Welch it could be said that he deserves commendation because many of the publications involved were distributed free of charge. The ostensible motives here, as in the case of the donation of royalties to charities, may well have been benign and even benevolent, but more basic considerations suggest acts that were far from unselfish.

---

[9] Out of consideration and respect for Admiral Rickover in connection with the controversy arising out of his copyrighting activities, Public Affairs Press placed no stress on the fact that he had sold to a private business firm exclusive rights to the contents of press releases issued by the Defense Department and the Atomic Energy Commission. In view, however, of the Admiral's insistence that the Press has challenged his copyrights because of crass considerations it should be pointed out that the editor of the Press stated as follows in a letter of November 11, 1958, to the Admiral:

"The fact that the royalties on your speeches are to be paid to the Crippled Children's Fund has nothing whatsoever to do with the basic issue at stake. It is certainly unselfish of you to make this stipulation, but I fail to see how freedom of press is advanced by royalties paid to the most laudable of charities through an arrangement that necessarily restricts freedom of press. Incidentally, we are not only willing to pay to the Crippled Children's Fund a sum equivalent to what your royalties would be if your speeches were private property, but also the profits derived from the sale of the book."

[10] Contrary to popular belief, nonprofit organizations are not automatically praiseworthy and unselfish. The most reprehensible of un-American activities are conducted by non-profit groups. And the most estimable of trade associations are non-profit bodies legitimately devoted to increasing the profits of their members.

3

CONSTITUTIONAL CONSIDERATIONS

Contrary to popular belief, the interests of the public, not the property rights of authors and publishers, constitute the fundamental basis of American copyright law.

The public benefit was the primary concern of the Founding Fathers when they authorized Congress to "promote the Progress of Science and useful Arts, by securing for limited Times to Authors and Inventors the exclusive Right to their respective Writings and Discoveries." As is plainly evident in this phrasing of the Constitution, *the paramount factor is promotion of the public welfare through "the Progress of Science and useful Arts."* Significantly, this consideration is subordinate to the basic purpose of the Constitution—to "promote the general welfare and secure the Blessings of Liberty to ourselves and our Posterity. . . "

In short, the Founding Fathers had the public benefit, *not the private benefit*, chiefly in mind when they placed in Congress permissive power to grant copyright privileges for limited periods. To them copyright was a means, not an end—a means which, *if properly used*, could help enrich the culture and knowledge of the nation. Conscious that copyright was in essence a private privilege to prevent the public from copying, a privilege to create a private monopoly conflicting with the public interest, they stipulated that it be granted subject to definite limitations.

In effect, the Constitutional authorization of copyright constituted a "contract or bargain"—an offer of limited property rights in return for contributions to the nation's culture and knowledge. This bargain recognized that those who made such contributions were entitled to suitable rewards for making the fruits of their *personal efforts* available to the public under restrictive circumstances.

It is doubtful in the extreme that the signers of the Constitution authorized copyrighting as a convenience for public servants. Considering their realistic attitude about the disadvantages of copyrighting and their evident desire to place "Writings and Discoveries" in the public domain as soon as practical [1] they could not possibly have countenanced copyrighting of or around officially derived knowledge about the vital interests of the nation. In the world they knew authors were for the most part

---

[1] Initially copyrights were restricted to a 14-year period; today they have a minimum life of 28 years and a maximum duration of 56 years.

men who drew solely upon their own resources in composing literary works for the edification and pleasure of their contemporaries. In the world of today a copyrighting public official, more often than not, has special access to vast and valuable collections of information made possible by the efforts of several million public servants and funds made available via taxes paid by 180 million Americans.

The basic democratic conception of American copyright was never more cogently expressed than in the report of the Congressional Committee recommending the adoption of the last extensive revision of the Copyright Law in 1909. The Committee was unambiguous:

"The enactment of copyright legislation by Congress under the terms of the Constitution is not based upon any natural right that the author has in his writings, for the Supreme Court has held that such rights as he has are purely statutory rights, but upon the ground that the welfare of the public will be served and progress of science and useful arts will be promoted by securing to authors for limited periods the exclusive rights to their writings. . .

"First, how much will the legislation stimulate the producer and so benefit the public; and second, how much will the monopoly granted be detrimental to the public? The granting of such exclusive rights, under the proper terms and conditions, confers a benefit upon the public that outweighs the evils of the temporary monopoly." [2]

It is to this Committee that the nation is indebted for the following provision in the Copyright Act:

'No copyright shall subsist in the original text of any work which is in the public domain, or in any work which was published in this country or any foreign country prior to July 1, 1909, and has not already been copyrighted in the United States, or in any publication of the United States Government, or any reprint, in whole or in part, thereof. . . "

This section of the Copyright Act prohibits copyrighting of works in the public domain because under the American conception of copyright, a conception confirmed by the artful phrasing of the Constitutional clause relating to copyright, the welfare of the public is best served by assuring the widest possible accessibility to works that are not and should not be the private property of any person or persons.

It is because of this conception that the American people today freely enjoy the fruits of writers like Shakespeare and Ralph Waldo Emerson, of composers like Mozart and Beethoven, of painters like Michaelangelo and Raphael, of statesmen like Jefferson and Lincoln. Were it not for this conception copyright claimants could play havoc with the works of these men. Performance of plays by Shakespeare would be subject to costly

[2] Report No. 2222, House of Representatives, 60th Congress, 2nd Session, 1909.

litigation. Reproduction of great paintings would be handicapped unfairly and unreasonably. Quoting Presidents Roosevelt and Eisenhower could be subject to special privilege, fee requirements, and even political preference.

TRUE PURPOSES OVERLOOKED

Extract from a statement by Luther H. Evans as the head of the Library of Congress and the Copyright Office.

"Copyright has a closer connection to today's world struggle than may be apparent at first to some who have not had occasion to consider the wider implications of the subject or may have been engrossed in the detailed problems of particular industries or interests. . . .

"The battle of ideas . . . [cannot] be long considered without questions being raised as to the nature of the rights of the creator and the length to which the state should go in extending its protection to all subsequent forms of reproduction of the original creation which in the English-speaking world are grouped under the name of 'copyright.'

"Misled in some measure by the numerous technically complicated details of the subject, many persons may have overlooked the fact that determination of sound copyright policies raises, alike in the domestic and the foreign field, the fundamental issues of our day: *avoidance of the evils of monopoly* with a minimum of state control; preservation of personal initiative with *greater equality of opportunity;* freedom and integrity of thought, speech, and *communication reconciled to media of mass communication.* Copyright properly understood and wisely handled may be at the same time a powerful stimulus to creation and the means of opening the channels of dissemination of thought, information and debate. *Misunderstood, and with its true purposes lost sight of, copyright can become a limitation on creation and a barrier to free interchange and expression.* Like many other products of man's genius in the realms both of science and of law, *copyright has a capacity for good or evil depending on his understanding and the use he makes of it.* (From *Copyright and the Public Interest* by Luther H. Evans, New York Public Library, 1949, pp. 3-5.)

Unfortunately, the basic principles of American copyright law have been neglected and disregarded in recent years. Except for espousals of them by Clement Bouve, head of the Copyright Office in the 1930's, Luther H. Evans, Librarian of Congress from 1945 to 1953, and L. B. Heilprin, an officer of the Council on Library Resources, they are conspicuous only by their absence from present day literature on copyright.[3]

Since much copyrighting by public officials is largely based upon the efforts of others in the government service and upon prodigious resources made possible by the nation's taxpayers, it is doubtful that such copyrighting complies with the originality and creativity requisites of the Copyright Act. The Constitutional authorization of the copyright and patent statutes specifically stipulates that authors and inventors may be granted exclusive rights for limited periods providing that they personally contribute to "the Progress of Science and useful Arts" through "their respective Writing and Discoveries."[4]

[3] See Copyright and the Public Interest, Luther Evans, New York Public Library (1949, 51 pages) and Copyright As Communication, L. B. Heilprin, Council on Library Resources (1959, 29 pages).

[4] See "Originality in the Law of Intellectual Property," Judge Leon R. Yankwich, U.S. District Court for the Southern District of California, Federal Rules Decisions, October, 1951.

4

RESTRICTION AND SUPPRESSION

Copyrighting by or through public officials is contrary to fundamental laws of the land. It can be and often is highly detrimental to the interests of the American people.

The First Amendment of the Constitution every public servant is sworn to uphold expressly forbids curtailment of freedom of press. Such freedom is substantially vitiated if public officials can place private restrictions on and around governmental information to which they have privileged access.

Section 8 of the U. S. Copyright Act specifically states: "No copyright shall subsist in any publication of the United States Government or any reprint, in whole or in part thereof." Despite this stipulation, incorporated into national law for the express purpose of preventing restrictions on government information, hundreds of public officials have placed private copyrights on an incredible amount of material that could not possibly be prepared without the benefit of official funds, resources and facilities. Despite this stipulation, copyright notices are placed even on publication bearing official seals and sold by the Government Printing Office. Despite, perhaps because of this stipulation, government officials have figured out scores of ways whereby a speech, article or book of a predominantly official nature can avoid being classified as a government publication

By virtue of the oath of office every public servant is required to take each owes the *utmost loyalty* to the Constitution and his employer, the American people. If this loyalty is to be meaningful, not meaningless, the personal interests and predilections of every official must be subordinate to his responsibilities to the American people. If his loyalty to the Constitution and to the nation should coincide with his personal values no conflict need arise. If, however, a conflict should arise—in the privacy of his thoughts or in the course of performing his duties—he has no choice but to resolve it in favor of the American people, not himself.

A government official should not violate or disregard the First Amendment through the copyright device or any other means. Of course, he can, if he so sees fit, copyright whatever he writes of a genuinely personal nature; that is his privilege. It is not, however, his privilege (or "right" via abuse of privilege) to place private copyright restrictions on and around officially derived knowledge, knowledge to which he has, as a public servant, special and exclusive access because of the public trust he holds. This is highly important for the following reasons:

The American government has in effect become the nation's bank of basic information. This bank is—or should be—operated by public trustees acting responsibly in behalf of the American people, not by private trustees acting in their own behalf.

As is amply evident in almost every sphere of American life—but especially in such highly important fields as atomic energy, astronautics, business and agriculture, medical research, and the sciences in general— governmental agencies and governmental funds are primary means of acquiring authoritative knowledge for the nation at large.

Without the benefit of vital governmental information the nation's economy would be chaotic. Indeed it is hard to believe that the United States could today enjoy its high standards of material living, its technological advances, or its confident sense of national security were it not for the enormous sums of money the American people contribute, via taxation, for the purpose of attaining the knowledge that make these things possible.

Manifestly it is not in the public interest for public officials to rampantly place private copyright restrictions on or around information to which they have privileged access as servants of the public.

What a man does with his own property is, of course, entirely his own business. In the case of writings that are unquestionably his own he is perfectly free to suppress them for all time,[1] withhold them from the public for years,[2] or sell them to the highest bidder who comes along tomorrow.

[1] What happened in connection with Oscar Wilde's "De Profundis" constitutes a perfect example of how copyright can be used to legalize suppression of a work. Last of Wilde's prose works, "De Profundis" was written in 1896 in the form of a letter to Lord Alfred Douglass. To clear his name of charges made by a Wilde biograher, Lord Alfred sought to publish "De Profundis" in the United States but was prevented from doing so by a friend of Wilde's who quickly printed 16 copies in New York, deposited one with the Library of Congress, sold one to an undisclosed person, and placed the remaining copies in a safe deposit vault until 1960. Today Wilde's friend could achieve copyright suppression without even going to the trouble of printing the book. Some pertinent details appeared in the Washington Post, January 3, 1960.

[2] Unintentional suppression exists on a large scale today because the Copyright Act appears to permit registration of a vast amount of material that is not printed, and that is not accessible to the public, and that is not even available for examination at the Library of Congress. The last is explained by the fact that the Library cannot possibly store everything that is copyrighted and must return or discard countless thousands of works. Moreover, only a small portion of copyrighted material is entered in the catalog cards furnished to the nation's libraries and filed in the reading rooms of the Library of Congress. Of 26 items copyrighted by Admiral Rick-

COPYRIGHT RESTRICTIONS ON SCHOLARSHIP

"At a recent informal meeting in Washington, representatives of several fields of science proposed a toast to the U. S. Copyright Law: 'May it go the way of the Volstead Act,' one said. These gentlemen by their toast were not proposing to deny to authors the fruit of their labors. But they were reflecting a growing sentiment on the part of scientists, scholars and researchers that *the present copyright law hinders rather than promotes the dissemination of scientific and scholarly information. . .*

"The scientists at the Washington meeting described some frustrating adventures they had had in trying to get permission to copy material they needed for their researches: cases of authors who held rights but could not be located by anyone, including their publishers; cases of publishers who had let books go out of print but nevertheless would not give permission to copy; and so on." (Publishers' Weekly, November 16, 1959)

*   *   *

"Researchers in many fields are demanding the right to copy and put to use copyright material without having to face the delays or the impossibility of obtaining permissions. *Our scientific progress, they say, is being balked by difficulties in obtaining the right to copy.*
"Industrial plants want to copy useful material out of books and periodicals to pass quickly around the plant. Teachers, especially at the graduate levels (and not only in fields of science), want to make multiple copies of chapters or articles; libraries of all types, public, college and industrial, are being asked for copies of materials from their shelves. . . .

"The interest of all these users is consistent with the public interest, but the desire to overstep the controls of copyright in order to avoid technicalities and delays brings up serious problems that are also matters of the public interest.

"How shall useful controls be maintained in the face of the rising demand for easy use? Many parties and also the public have an interest in an informed, just and workable solution." (Publishers' Weekly, May 30, 1960)

For every public official who places copyright restrictions on official material he happens to consider his private property there may well be scores who feel they are fully justified in suppressing "official" matter they consider their "private" property.[3]

It is not generally realized that under the present terms of the Copyright Act the validity, *not the invalidity*, of a challenged copyright often depends upon proof that the author withheld and/or restricted distribution of a work prior to copyrighting. The greater the proof of withholding and/or restricted distribution, the greater the chances of securing copyright protection. Hence a public official desirous of securing an unchallengeable copyright on material he considers his own must first make sure that it is effectively hidden from the public before he applies for copyright registration.

Ironically enough, it was on the ground that Rickover had restricted distribution of texts of his speeches that the Federal District Court held that all of his copyrights were valid. The U. S. Court of Appeals felt, on the other hand, that the evidence was to the contrary in regard to most of the speeches and that only in the case of several speeches was there enough proof of withholding to warrant validation of copyright.

In ruling that he was satisfied Admiral Rickover had "restricted distribution" of his speeches, Judge Holtzoff declared: "It is well established that a restricted distribution of a limited number of copies does not constitute . . . a dedication to the public. It does not bar the author from later procuring a copyright when the product is actually published." In the case of Werckmeister v. American Lithograph Company[4] Judge Holtzoff pointed out, this doctrine was "formulated and applied" by the Court of Appeals for the Second Circuit, in the following terms:

"Publication of a subject of copyright is effected by its communication or dedication to the public. Such a publication is what is known as a 'general publication.' There may be also a 'limited publication.' The use of the word 'publication' in these two senses is unfortunate and has led to much confusion. A limited publication of a subject of copyright is one which communicates a knowledge of its contents under conditions expressly or impliedly *precluding its dedication to the public*. . .

"The nature of the property in question in large measure determines the extent of the public right . . . The exhibition or private circulation

---

over as of the beginning of October 1960, for example, only one was listed in the reading card files; the remainder were for all practical purposes unknown and inaccessible to the public.

[3] Destroying or hiding are, of course, the simplest and most convenient means whereby an official can suppress or withhold whatever he considers his own property.

[4] 134 Fed. 321, 324, 325.

THREAT TO THE ADVANCE OF SCIENCE

There is "an actual and impending crisis in scientific communication. Copyright law operates as a control on important dissemination channels. Instead of fulfilling its original purpose of fostering science (a purpose amply fulfilled in the case of the arts) *copyright law is now actually threatening the advance of science.*

"It is . . . a matter of public concern to find that *the operation of the copyright law has not been as beneficent toward science as it has been toward the arts.* In the early days of copyright this effect was not important enough to be noticed. Scientific communication took place by letter, by word of mouth, by book, and in general through more personal means than it does today. Today the chief channel of scientific communication is the journal article. While there is still much word of mouth communication, and some private writing and distribution of prepublication results, the great mass of ideas are disseminated through the journals. Progress in science therefore depends on unrestricted dissemination of these articles. . .

"Legal use of even a small part of a copyrighted article requires permission. Sometimes this is readily obtained. But the general experience is otherwise. Since there exists no specific machinery which connects those who wish to copy scholarly material with those holding copyrights, the delays and the expense involved in copying are prohibitive. It has been repeatedly demonstrated that the time consumed in writing, the uncertainty of getting a reply, the number of authorities to whom requests must be addressed, and the impossibility of securing uniform acceptance, usually render an even moderate-sized copying enterprise unprofitable. *The threat of suit for infringement is always present, and too great to risk.* This applies particularly to libraries, the recipients of most of the requests for photoduplication . . . The same situation exists in a majority of Government agencies, which adhere more or less strictly to the law. In the Commerce Department it is against the rules to photostat a news clipping. In many industries the same narrow rule is observed. Result: *there is a large attenuation in the potential circulation of scientific information.* How large is not possible to estimate. The fact is certain, however, that there exist large areas of scientific communication which are neglected or left alone"—Extracts from *Copyright As Communication* by L. B. Heilprin, 1959.

of the original or of printed copies is not a publication, unless it amounts to a general offer to the public."

Although the decision reached in the Werckmeister case had stressed that "The nature of the property in question in large measure determines the extent of the public right," Judge Holtzoff neglected to point out that this case had involved the exhibition of paintings by an obscure artist to a small group of persons, whereas the Rickover case involved statements on the defense and security of the nation as set forth by one of the nation's highest officials in a government press release.

Not generally known is the fact that inconspicuous suppression can be effectively achieved through copyright procedures. Under these procedures a registrant can secure a binding copyright merely by averring (no proof is necessary) that copies of his work have been placed upon public sale. Whether the number of copies allegedly placed on sale was as small as 5 or as large as 5,000 makes no difference. Nor does it matter whether a work is placed on sale in the middle of Lake Michigan or in a Times Square bookstore.

In defense of copyrighting by public officials it is sometimes pointed out that it is not their desire to prevent "reasonable" quotation of their "private" works. No doubt this is usually sincerely meant. The trouble is that *the public has no way of knowing that it is meant;* nor does the public have any way of gauging intent — a variable subject to change without notice at the will or whim of the copyright claimant.

The copyright notice in most books is invariably accompanied by the following typical warning:[1] "No part of this book may be reproduced in any form without permission in writing from the publisher, except by a reviewer wishing to quote brief passages in connection with a review written for inclusion in a magazine or newspaper or broadcast."[2]

This notice means that quotation is permitted solely for publicity and sales promotion purposes.

The following variation appears in an official Army history published by the Government Printing Office and sold by the Superintendent of Documents: "All rights in this book are reserved. This book or any part thereof may not be reproduced without written authorization from: The Chief of Military History, Department of the Army, Washington 25, D. C."[3]

[1] The copyright notices in works published by Public Affairs Press have at no time been accompanied by such strictures. Its policy in this regard differs from that of most book publishers.

[2] From page 4 of compilation of Rickover speeches published under his personal copyright by a New York firm in 1959. The statement was fully justified from the firm's viewpoint in that it had purchased exclusive rights to the speeches. Almost all of the contents of the work were based upon press releases issued by the Defense Department and the Atomic Energy Commission.

[3] This notice appears on page ii of the exhibit on page 46.

COPYRIGHT AS A BLOCK TO PROGRESS

"The protection given the copyright-owner should not stifle independent creation by others. Nobody else should market the author's book, but we refuse to say nobody else should use it. The world goes ahead because each of us builds on the work of our predecessors. 'A dwarf standing on the shoulders of a giant can see farther than the giant himself.' Progress would be stifled if the author had a complete monopoly of everything in his book for fifty-six years or any other long period. Some use of its contents must be permitted in connection with the independent creation of other authors. The very policy which leads the law to encourage his creativeness also justifies it in facilitating the creativeness of others."—Zechariah Chafee, Jr., in "Reflections on the Law of Copyright," Columbia Law Review, 45, 503, 1945.

Among the works officially listed and publicized as a government document is a book that contains the following unusual warning:

"All rights reserved. No part of this book may be reproduced in any form or by any mechanical means, including mimeograph and tape recorder, without permission in writing from the publisher." [4]

If this precedent is followed the day may not be distant when a copyright notice will say: "No portion of this work can be quoted in conversation heard by more than two persons." This isn't at all far fetched. The contents of speeches have long been subject to the Copyright Act.

An eminent jurist who has long championed the rights of the public in his rulings on copyright issues, Judge Leon R. Yankwich, Judge of the U.S. District Court for the Southern District of California, aptly particularized the problem with these words:

"For a long time I have had the conviction that writers in the fields of ideas—political, social, scientific and other—have been cowed into the belief that a reasonable use of copyrighted materials of others in the same field is not safe without permission from the owners of the copyright, and that, in this manner, reasonable access to such materials, in the interest of progress of ideas, is being discouraged and impediments are placed in the path of the scholar and writer in these fields.

"The condition has been aided by the policy adopted by publishers of inserting, after the copyright notice, statements in substance as follows:

---

[4] This notice appears in "Command Decisions", a work "prepared by the Office of the Chief of Military History, Department of the Army" and publicized by the Army and the Government Printing Office as an official document.

'All rights in this book are reserved. No part of the book may be used or reproduced in any manner whatsoever without written permission except in the case of brief quotations embodied in critical articles and reviews. For information address Smudgefree Printers, Inc., 1075 Oak Mill Lane, Copenhagen Wisconsin.' " [5]

Anyone who quotes a copyrighted work without express authorization proceeds at his own risk.[6] If he cites merely a paragraph or two without securing formal permission to do so, permission customarily subject to payment of fees and/or other stipulations, he is guilty of committing an act in violation of the copyright notice. While it is true than an act of this sort is not likely to land him in trouble if his infringement of copyright is negligible, he has no assurances whatsoever as to this.

The fact is that the "fair use" concept—a concept often cited in behalf of "reasonable" quotation of copyrighted matter used without authorization—*has no statutory sanction.* At best it is a variable with many risks and uncertainties.

The fact is that the Copyright Act does not contain any statement as to what "fair use" may be made of copyrighted works. Nor does it indicate permissible usages. While it spells out in detail the various rights of the copyright owner, it does not even suggest wherein those rights may be inconsequentially infringed. By its terms *the registered claimant has full authority to take legal action against anyone who infringes in any way any of the rights granted by the law.*

The fact is that the Rickover copyright case arose out of the *Admiral's refusal to permit so much as a sentence to be quoted* [7] from speeches issued as official press releases of the Defense Department and the Atomic Energy Commission. He prohibited quotation in any way, without knowing whether Public Affairs Press desired to cite a paragraph or a page and without even inquiring as to how or where quotation might be used.[8]

The fact is that although phrasing of the Press' suit against the Admiral specifically asked the U.S. District Court to rule on whether

[5] "What Is Fair Use?", by Leon R. Yankwich, University of Chicago Law Review, Autumn, 1954, p. 203.

[6] The same risk applies even to photostating a page from a copyrighted work. Note exhibit on page 35. For details see "Photocopying by Libraries and Copyright", Miles O. Price, Professor of Law, Columbia University, in Library Trends, January, 1960, and "The Copying of Literary Property in Library Collections", Louis C. Smith, Senior Attorney of the Copyright Office, Law Library Journal, August, 1953, and August, 1954, issues.

[7] Letter of October 31, 1958, letterhead of the Atomic Energy Commission.

[8] In the historic decision in the case of Millar V. Taylor, a decision that laid the groundwork for copyrighting in Britain, Lord Chief Justice Mansfield warned that this device was justifiable if "the world may not be deprived of improvements, nor the progress of the arts be retarded." 1769, 4 Burrows Reports 2303.

he could prevent quotation of his speeches in whole or in part, *the ruling of the Court did not permit such quotation.* And while the superior Court's decision left the door open to possible quotation of several speeches it considered under valid copyright, it held that *the nature and extent of quotation was subject to specific judicial authorization.*

When toward the climax of the Congressional exposure of rigged television quiz shows in the winter of 1959 a scoop article by one of its investi-

---

U.S. DEPARTMENT OF COMMERCE
DICTA ON COPYRIGHTS

Extracts from an official bulletin entitled "Reproduction of Copyrighted Material."

"Permission to reproduce copyrighted material is required under the U. S. Copyright Law and if it cannot be obtained it is safer not to use the material. Without such permission, *even limited reproduction of copyrighted material for internal use* may violate copyright protection.

"Mere acknowledgment of a copyrighted source does not avoid legal liability. . . .

"All requisitions for reproduction of copyrighted material by *Photocopy, mimeograph or other exact-copy processes* shall be accompanied by a statement from the copyright owner granting permission for such reproduction or written certification that such permission has been granted. . . .

"Copyrightable material encompasses a wide range of subject matter, including but not limited to books, periodicals, unpublished lectures, maps, drawings, photographs, prints etc. . . .

"Where foreign works are concerned, it is not possible to give any general guides to identification of copyrighted material. . . .

"In general, unauthorized reproduction of any . . . material part of a work . . . that is protected by copyright constitutes infringement. . . .

"No clearcut line can be drawn to indicate the extent to which one may quote or extract from copyrighted work without infringement." (January 27, 1956).

SECTION 201.2(d)

of the

Regulations of the Copyright Office

(In effect as of June 18, 1959)

Requests for Copies.

(1) Requests for additional certificates of registration should be sent to the Copyright Office, and the accompanying fees should be made payable to the Register of Copyrights.

(2) Requests for photocopies of copyright deposits, official correspondence, and Copyright Office records (other than additional certificates of registration) should be sent to the Chief, Photoduplication Service, Library of Congress, Washington 25, D. C., the accompanying fees in payment of such services being made payable to that official. When the photocopy is to be certified by the Copyright Office, the additional certification fee should be made payable to the Register of Copyrights and both remittances together with the transmittal letter are to be sent to the Copyright Office.

(3) Requests for photocopies of official correspondence shall identify the specific material desired and shall contain a statement enabling the Copyright Office to determine if the writer is properly and directly concerned.

(4) Requests for photocopies of copyright deposits will be granted when one or more of the following conditions are fulfilled:

(i) **Authorization by owner.** When authorized in writing by the copyright owner or his designated agent.

(ii) **Request by attorney.** When required in connection with litigation, actual or prospective, in which the copyrighted work is involved; but in all such cases the attorney representing the actual or prospective plaintiff or defendant for whom the request is made shall give in writing: (a) The names of the parties and the nature of the controversy; (b) the name of the court where the action is pending, or, in the case of a prospective proceeding, a full statement of the facts of the controversy in which the copyrighted work is involved; and (c) satisfactory assurances that the requested copy will be used only in connection with the specified litigation.

(iii) **Court order.** When an order to have the copy made is issued by a court having jurisdiction of a case in which the copy is to be submitted as evidence.

In essence it says that you can't obtain a photostat (or other type of reproduction) of so much as a page in any book under copyright—unless you have written authorization from the copyright owner or his agent or can attest to necessity because of litigation pending before a court. These restrictions apply to government agencies as well as individuals. By virtue of such regulations an employee of the United States who copyrights official intelligence he feels he came by in his private capacity can require the U. S. Government to pay him for the privilege of using material that very Government made possible. Above are Library of Congress regulations.

gators, Richard N. Goodwin, appeared in Life magazine, the Fourth Estate sensed quite clearly the dangers of withholding by "inside" officials for "outside" purposes.

Under the heading "Public Information For Sale", the Washington News ran the following editorial on November 12:

"It may be merely a coincidence. But newsmen here assigned to the TV investigation say they had a lot of trouble this fall getting any information out of the investigating staff. Several reporters were told Chairman Oren Harris of the House committee had given orders—no interviews.

"Anyway, it now develops that one of the staffers, Richard N. Goodwin, classified as a consultant, has sold his own 'inside' story to a weekly magazine. Rep. Harris is quoted as saying he o.k.'ed this arrangement providing Mr. Goodwin didn't discuss the work of the committee. What else did he have to discuss? The whole article is about the committee's inquiry.

"It is no skin off our nose — we have had ample coverage of the TV scandal. But we thought this investigation was being run to provide information to the public, not information to be hoarded up for private sale.

"The Harris committee has set up itself as a kind of public conscience over the television industry, and other areas of mischief. The Goodwin deal doesn't seem to jibe."

In an editorial entitled "Question of Propriety" the Washington Post commented:

"The question is whether it is proper for an official still employed by a congressional committee to sell for his personal profit information he has accumulated as an investigator for the Committee.

"We think that it would be quite improper for a United States attorney to write a magazine article on a sensational case that he was prosecuting. Why? Because he ought to be concerned solely with laying the unadorned facts before the court. The same is true of a congressional investigator. If he is thinking about building up a story that will attract a national magazine, he is in danger of slipping into the frame of mind of a showman or exploiter. . . .

"Another question that ought to be asked is whether an investigator who collects a fee from one magazine can be wholly impartial in making information available to all other news media. Perhaps Mr. Goodwin can achieve such impartiality, but in the circumstances it will be difficult to convince others that he is a wholly disinterested finder of facts and dispenser of information. In a sensitive public position the appearance of objectivity and lack of personal interest are almost as important as the fact."

HEADQUARTERS ARMY SERVICE FORCES
WASHINGTON 25, D. C.

SPMSE 350 (2 MAY 45)   4 MAY 1945

Mr. M. B. Schnapper, Executive Secretary
American Council on Public Affairs
2153 Florida Avenue, Northwest
Washington 8, D. C.

Dear Mr. Schnapper:

This is a reply to your letter of 2 May, in which you
inquire whether a copyright notice will appear in those copies
of GI Roundtable pamphlets to be made available to the public
by the Superintendent of Documents.

No copyright notice will be included in GI Roundtable
pamphlets offered for sale by the Superintendent of Documents.
It is believed that, once an authoritative and complete edition
of the pamphlets is thus accessible to the public, the copyright
protection against possible distortion or misrepresentation of
the material will no longer be essential.

With regard to your offer to assist in the promotion of
the pamphlets, it is suggested that this is a matter which you
might properly propose to the Superintendent of Documents.

Sincerely yours,

FRANCIS T. SPAULDING
Colonel, AUS
Chief, Army Education Branch
Information and Education Division

Note the date—May 4, 1945. It was in the spring of that year
that the author began his 15 year fight to stop copyrighting of
official material. Significantly, the letter concedes the Army
had used the copyright device not because private material was
involved but, as Colonel Spaulding admits, as a means of preventing "possible distortion or misrepresentation". In short,
copyright was employed to avoid possibly unfavorable publicity.
Previously the Colonel was favorably disposed toward granting
copyright permission if complete texts would be reprinted. Usually
copyright owners insist that no more than extracts be used.
Admiral Rickover has objected to quotation of his speeches in
whole or in part except if publicity is advantageous.

GI ROUNDTABLE SUBJECTS

INTRODUCTORY COPIES of each new *GI Roundtable* pamphlet are automatically issued to information-education officers in the United States and oversea areas. Additional copies are authorized on the basis of one copy for each 25 military personnel. Pamphlets may be requisitioned from the United States Armed Forces Institute, Madison 3, Wisconsin, or from the nearest USAFI Oversea Branch. List EM number, title, and quantity. New subjects will be announced as published. *GI Roundtable* subjects now available:

EM 1, GUIDE FOR DISCUSSION LEADERS
EM 2, WHAT IS PROPAGANDA?
EM 10, WHAT SHALL BE DONE ABOUT GERMANY AFTER THE WAR?
EM 11, WHAT SHALL BE DONE WITH THE WAR CRIMINALS?
EM 12, CAN WE PREVENT FUTURE WARS?
EM 13, HOW SHALL LEND-LEASE ACCOUNTS BE SETTLED?
EM 14, IS THE GOOD NEIGHBOR POLICY A SUCCESS?
EM 15, WHAT SHALL BE DONE ABOUT JAPAN AFTER VICTORY?
EM 20, WHAT HAS ALASKA TO OFFER POSTWAR PIONEERS?
EM 22, WILL THERE BE WORK FOR ALL?
EM 23, WHY CO-OPS? WHAT ARE THEY? HOW DO THEY WORK?
EM 24, WHAT LIES AHEAD FOR THE PHILIPPINES?
EM 27, WHAT IS THE FUTURE OF TELEVISION?
EM 30, CAN WAR MARRIAGES BE MADE TO WORK?*
EM 31, DO YOU WANT YOUR WIFE TO WORK AFTER THE WAR?
EM 32, SHALL I BUILD A HOUSE AFTER THE WAR?
EM 33, WHAT WILL YOUR TOWN BE LIKE?
EM 34, SHALL I GO BACK TO SCHOOL?
EM 35, SHALL I TAKE UP FARMING?
EM 36, DOES IT PAY TO BORROW?
EM 37, WILL THERE BE A PLANE IN EVERY GARAGE?
EM 40, WILL THE FRENCH REPUBLIC LIVE AGAIN?
EM 41, OUR BRITISH ALLY
EM 42, OUR CHINESE ALLY
EM 43, THE BALKANS—MANY PEOPLES, MANY PROBLEMS
EM 44, AUSTRALIA: OUR NEIGHBOR "DOWN UNDER"
EM 45, WHAT FUTURE FOR THE ISLANDS OF THE PACIFIC?
EM 46, OUR RUSSIAN ALLY
EM 90, GI RADIO ROUNDTABLE

---

* For distribution in United States only.

☆ U. S. GOVERNMENT PRINTING OFFICE: 1946—673396

For sale by the Superintendent of Documents, U. S. Government Printing Office
Washington 25, D. C. - Price 15 cents

A list of Army pamphlets removed from copyright restriction at the insistence of the editor of Public Affairs Press. A score of other pamphlets was in the series. (For details see previous page).

5

EXAMPLES OF COPYRIGHTING BY AND THROUGH GOVERNMENT AGENCIES AND OFFICIALS

In one way or another officials[1] of virtually every agency have been directly and indirectly party to the copyrighting of official information in one way or another and at one time or another in recent years. However, it would appear that the copyrighting zeal of officials of the armed forces—particularly top echelon officers of the Army, the Navy and the Air Force—is far greater and more ingenious than that of officials of other agencies.

Viewed in the light of the Department of Defense Directive entitled "Clearance of Department of Defense Public Information", a great deal of copyrighting by and through officers of the Army, Navy, and Air Force is of a distinctly questionable nature. This Directive states:

"The people of the United States are properly interested in the Department of Defense and the steps it is taking to protect the national security. *The Department of Defense has an obligation to inform the public with respect to the Department's activities* and to provide the public with accurate, factual and other proper information regarding the Army, Navy, Air Force and Marine Corps. Public access shall be limited only by restrictions imposed in the national interest pursuant to law in order to safeguard information requiring protection in the interest of national defense . . .

"Information provided should be timely and presented to the public through the usual news media (press, magazines, journals, radio, television, etc.) in a manner consistent with the ethics and procedures normally followed in dealing with such media.

"Defense information originated by the Department of Defense or any of its agencies for official release to the public through news media by military or civilian personnel of the Department of Defense, such as official speeches, press releases, and photographic material, shall be submitted to the Secretary of Defense through the Assistant Secretary of Defense (Public Affairs) or other designees for review and clearance . . .

[1] More often than not officials register or transfer their copyrights or grant exclusive publishing rights in their private capacities. For obvious reasons these acts are rarely (if ever) performed in their official capacities. In view of the prohibitions of the Copyright Act copyrighting by an official in his official capacity would patently undermine the validity of his registration. For the same reason, registration is sometimes filed privately but in behalf of a government agency.

CONSTRAINT BY COPYRIGHT

"Military and civilian personnel shall not make any commitment to furnish official manuscripts to any outside publication unless prior clearance is obtained from the appropriate Secretary of a military department, and the Secretary of Defense or their designees. *All such official manuscripts on military matters written by military and civilian personnel for outside publication shall be submitted for review and clearance* by the appropriate Secretary of a military department and the Secretary of Defense or their designees, before submission to the publisher or editor.

"Material originating within the Department of Defense shall not be cleared for public release until it is *reviewed for . . . conflict with established policies or programs of the Department of Defense, or those of the national Government . . .*

"Personnel of the Department of Defense, military and civilian, who write for outside publication not in connection with their official duties on any subject or in any form shall ascertain that such activity will not interfere or conflict in any way with their regularly assigned duties. *Such activity will not be conducted during normal working hours, or accomplished with the use of Department of Defense facilities, or personnel.* Such writers will be on an exact parity with outside professional writers with respect to accessibility and use of technical or other information for manuscripts or articles written for publication. Articles by such personnel, dealing with military matters, will be submitted to the Office of Security Review, OASD(PA), for review and clearance to avoid any possible violation of military security." [2]

To what extent were works cited in the accompanying pages prepared for "outside publication"? Should officially prepared military histories printed by the Government Printing Office and sold by the Superintendent of Documents be considered within the term "outside publication"? Is copyrighting of this and similar material not in "conflict" with the prohibitions of the Copyright Act? If such material contains information to which military personnel have privileged access are their writers "on an exact parity with outside professional writers" or the public at large?

Similar questions can be asked with reference to copyrighting that does not appear to be consistent with the Navy regulations regarding "Disclosure and Publication of Information":

"No person in the Naval Establishment shall convey or disclose by oral or written communication, publication, or other means, except as may be required by his official duties, any information whatever concerning the Naval or other Military Establishment or forces, or any person, thing, plan, or measure pertaining thereto . . . except by proper naval authority

---

[2] Directive No. 52,309, August 17, 1957.

September 10, 1959

Dear Mr. Schnapper:

Secretary McElroy has asked me to reply to your letter of September 1, 1959. In it you enclosed a copy of your letter to the Editor of the New York Times supporting the Secretary's decision refusing permission to General Thomas S. Power, Commanding General of the Strategic Air Command, to publish commercially, through private and exclusive contract, a book dealing with national defense plans, policies and programs.

The Secretary appreciates your support and has asked me to advise you that he completely agrees with your view to the effect that such refusal does not involve any aspect whatsoever of inter- ference with freedom of the press or suppression of public infor- mation.

It is believed that such confusion as may exist in this matter arises from a failure to distinguish between two situations: The Department's official public information responsibilities and a situation which is presented by proposed private exclusive com- mercial publication by key civilian or military officials of articles or books dealing with national defense plans, policies or programs.

As to the first situation, and as your letter to the TIMES notes, there is no prohibition against such officials making their views publicly known via official publications, television, radio, press interviews, press conferences, press releases, testimony before Congressional Committees, etc.

As to the matter of private writings by Department personnel, it has been the established policy of the Department for years that key civilian and military officials may not as private individuals author for exclusive publication, articles or books dealing with national defense plans, policies or programs except for publication in official or unofficial Service Journals and in recognized scientific or professional magazines, journals, encyclopedias and the like.

Portion of a letter from Assistant Secretary of Defense Murray Snyder. In explaining the Defense Department's position regarding "private and exclusive" publication by government officers, he states that "key civilian and military officials may not as private individuals author for exclusive publication, articles or books dealing with national defense" except in cases of the type mentioned.

(Letter is continued on the next page.)

Among the reasons for this policy are: the need to insure the right of the general public to have access to official information through the normally accepted public information media sources and without the payment of substantial tolls for it; the need to avoid favoring one publication over its competitors; the need to prevent Government personnel from unfairly competing with outside professional writers on the basis of their superior access to inside information; the need to avoid real or apparent commercialization of official positions; and the need to avoid actions by personnel which could conflict with or interfere with their ability to perform official duties or be prejudicial to morale or discipline or otherwise be incompatible with the responsibilities of the Department and its personnel.

The policy of the Department of Defense has always been that it has an affirmative obligation to provide the public with the maximum information as to its activities, consistent with national security. Included in this obligation is the serious responsibility to do so through the usual public information media on an equitable basis without favoritism or other discrimination. It has been the experience of the Department that the policy concerning the authoring of books and articles by key civilian or military personnel on defense plans, policies or programs contributes to the fulfillment of our public information responsibilities. We believe that the policy is in the public interest.

A copy of Department of Defense Directive 5230.9, which reflects the basic policies pertaining to this matter, is enclosed in accordance with your request.

Sincerely,

Murray Snyder

Enclosure – DoD Directive 5230.9·

. . . nor shall any person in the naval service make any public speech or permit publication of any article written by or for him which is prejudicial to the interests of the United States.

"No person in the Naval Establishment shall, other than in the discharge of his official duties, disclose any information whatever, whether classified or nonclassified, or whether obtained from official records or within the knowledge of the relator, which might aid or be of assistance in the prosecution or support of any claim against the United States. (See act of June 25, 1948, ch. 645, sec. 1 §283, 62 Stat. 697, as amended; 18 U.S.C. 283.)

"Persons in the naval service desiring to publish articles on professional, political, or international subjects in accordance with the provisions of this regulation shall cause their signatures to appear on such articles, *together with a statement to the effect that the opinions or assertions contained therein are the private ones of the writer and are not to be construed as official or reflecting the views of the Navy Department or the naval service at large* . . .

"No person in the naval service . . . assigned to duty in connection with the public relations activities of the Naval Establishment shall receive any compensation for acting as . . . correspondent, commentator, or analyst.

"*Subject to the requirements and restrictions of this article,* persons in the naval service are at liberty to publish articles without further permission from higher authority."[3]

Judging by the nature of much of the material cited in the pages that follow a great deal of it—especially works concerning military affairs, atomic energy, astronautics, etc—must have been subject to official secrecy classification while in process of preparation. It is difficult to believe that it is customary to place such classification on purely personal private property of public officials.

[3] Article 1252 of U.S. Navy Regulations, 1948.

CONSTRAINT BY COPYRIGHT

OFFICIAL MILITARY HISTORIES
COPYRIGHTED BY ARMY OFFICERS

All of these books were printed by the Government Printing Office and are available from the Superintendent of Documents. The official seal of the United States is imprinted on the cover of each. The copyright claimants had the rank of General and were Chief of the Office of Military History at about the period of copyright registration. However, the official status of the copyright claimants is not indicated in the copyright notices.

The Organization and Role of the Army Service Forces, by John D. Millett. (1954, 494 pp., $4.25). Copyrighted by Albert C. Smith.
The Fall of the Philippines, by Louis Morton. (1953, 626 pp., $5.25). Copyrighted by Orlando Ward.
Victory in Papua, by Samuel Milner. (1957, 409 pp., $6.00). Copyrighted by R. W. Stephens.
Seizure of the Gilberts and Marshalls, by Philip A. Crowl and Edmund G. Love. (1955, 414 pp., $5.75). Copyrighted by Albert C. Smith.
The Approach to the Philippines, by Robert Ross Smith. (1953, 623 pp., $6.25). Copyrighted by Orlando Ward.
Northwest Africa: Seizing the Initiative in the West, by George F. Howe. (1957, 748 pp., $7.75). Copyrighted by Richard W. Stephens.
The Lorraine Campaign, by H. M. Cole. (1950, 657 pp., $11.00). Copyrighted by Orlando Ward.
The Supreme Command, by Forrest C. Pogue. (1954, 607 pp., $6.50). Copyrighted by Albert C. Smith.
Logistical Support of the Armies, Vol. I (May 1941-September 1944) by Roland G. Ruppenthal. (1953, 616 pp., $4.50). Copyrighted by Orlando Ward.
Logistical Support of the Armies, Vol. II (September 1944-May 1945) by Roland G. Ruppenthal. (1959, 540, 540 pp., $4.50). Copyrighted by R. W. Stephens.
Time Runs Out in CBI, by Charles F. Romanus and Riley Sunderland. (1959, 428 pp.) Copyrighted by Richard W. Stephens.
Rearming the French, by Marcel Vigneras. (1957, 444 pp., $4.25). Copyrighted by John H. Stokes.
Chief of Staff: Prewar Plans and Preparations, by Mark Skinner Watson. (1950, 551 pp., $4.25). Copyrighted by Orlando Ward.
Washington Command Post: The Operations Division, by Ray S. Cline. (1951, 413 pp., $3.75). Copyrighted by Orlando Ward.
Strategic Planning for Coalition Warfare, by Maurice Matloff and Edwin

Publications

of

OFFICE

CHIEF OF

MILITARY

HISTORY

DEPARTMENT OF THE

ARMY

MILITARY INSTRUCTION

WASHINGTON, D.C.

Title page of an Army bulletin listing as official
works more than a score of military documents
copyrighted by various high officers.

UNITED STATES ARMY IN WORLD WAR II

The War in the Pacific

VICTORY IN PAPUA

by

Samuel Milner

OFFICE OF THE CHIEF OF MILITARY HISTORY
DEPARTMENT OF THE ARMY
WASHINGTON, D. C., 1957

Title page of one of the official military histories
printed by the Government Printing Office under
copyrights of Army officers.

This copyright notice appears in "Victory in Papua".
R. W. Stephens was Assistant Chief of the Office of
Military History at about the time of copyright.

M. Snell. (1953, 454 pp., $3.75). Copyrighted by Orlando Ward.

Global Logistics and Strategy, by Richard M. Leighton and Robert W. Coakley. (1955, 780 pp., $6.25). Copyrighted by Albert C. Smith.

The Army and Economic Mobilization, by R. Elberton Smith. (1958, 749 pp., $5.25). Copyrighted by Richard W. Stephens.

Guadalcanal: The First Offensive, by John Miller, Jr. (1949, 413 pp., $4.00). Copyrighted by Orlando Ward.

Cross-Channel Attack, by Gordon A. Harrison. (1951, 519 pp., $6.75). Copyrighted by Orlando Ward.

The Persian Corridor and Aid to Russia, by T. H. Vail Motter. (1952, 545 pp., $4.00). Copyrighted by Orlando Ward.

Stillwell's Mission to China, by Charles F. Romanus and Riley Sunderland. (1953, 441 pp., $5.50). Copyrighted by Orlando Ward.

Stillwell's Command Problems, by Charles F. Romanus and Riley Sunderland. (1956, 518 pp., $6.25). Copyrighted by Albert C. Smith.

The Signal Corps, by Dulany Terrett. (1956, 383 pp., $3.50). Copyrighted by Albert C. Smith.

The Transportation Corps: Responsibilities, Organization, and Operations, by Chester Wardlow. (1951, 454 pp., $3.75). Copyrighted by Orlando Ward.

Three Battles: Arnaville, Altuzzo, and Schmidt, by Charles B. MacDonald and Sidney T. Mathews. (1952, 443 pp., $4.50). Copyrighted by Orlando Ward.

The Women's Army Corps, by Mattie E. Treadwell. (1954, 841 pp., $6.25). Copyrighted by Orlando Ward.

The Quartermaster Corps: Organization, Supply, and Services, Vol. I, by Erna Risch. (1953, 418 pp., $3.75). Copyrighted by Orlando Ward.

The Quartermaster Corps: Organization, Supply, and Services, Vol. II, by Erna Risch and Chester L. Kieffer. (1955, 433 pp., $4.00). *Not copyrighted. In what respect is it different from Vol. I?*

*   *   *

Command Decisions, Kent Roberts Greenfield, editor. Listed as an official work in "Publications of the Office, Chief of Military History, Department of the Army". Copyrighted by Harcourt, Brace and Company in 1959. Mr. Greenfield was Chief Army Historian in 1959.

UNITED STATES NAVAL INSTITUTE BOOKS

Are their copyrights valid? Are the contents of each truly private? Which works were commissioned by the Navy De-

partment? Which by other military services? Which were privately prepared? Does the Navy prefer publishing through the Institute because Government Printing Office publications are not legally copyrightable?

A private, non-profit association of more than 55,000 members, the United States Naval Institute was formed in 1873 for "the advancement of professional, literary, and scientific knowledge in the Navy".

In a description of its publishing activities the Institute states that it "serves as the university press for the Seagoing services." For a complete list of Institute publications see its 18-page catalog in "The Publishers' Trade List Annual, 1960."

How to Survive on Land and Sea, by Office of Chief of Naval Operations, U.S. Navy. (Copyrighted 1943 and 1951 by the U.S. Naval Institute, 366 pp., $4.00).

Air Operations in Naval Warfare, edited by Commander Walter C. Blattmann, USN. (1957, 192 pp., $2.00).

The Bluejackets' Manual, U.S. Navy, by Captain J. V. Noel, Jr., USN. (Fifteenth edition, 1957; reprinted 1959, 648 pp., $1.95).

The Coast Guardsman's Manual, by Captain W. C. Hogan, USCG. (Revised by Lieutenant Commander M. M. Dickinson, USCG, assisted by Loran W. Behrens, BMC, USN-FR.) (Third edition, 1958, 830 pp., $4.00).

Division Officer's Guide, by Captain J. V. Noel, Jr. (Fourth edition, 1959, 304 pp., $2.25).

Elementary Seamanship, prepared by Lieutenant Commander Maurice C. Hartle, USN, Lieutenant Charles M. Lake, USN, Lieutenant Harry P. Maders, USN, and J. J. Metzger, BMC, USN. (1958, 92 pp., $2.00).

Elements of Applied Thermodynamics, by Captain W. A. Brockett, USN and R. M. Johnston, and A. E. Bock. (Third revised edition, 1958, 496 pp., $5.00).

Fundamentals of Construction and Stability of Naval Ships, by Thomas C. Gilmer, U.S. Naval Academy. (Second edition, 1959, 370 pp., $5.50).

International Law for Naval Officers, by Commander C. C. Soule, USN and Lieutenant Commander C. McCauley, USN. (Revised by Lieutenant Commander C. J. Bright, USN, 245 pp., $2.00).

International Law for Seagoing Officers, by Commander Burdick H. Brittin, USN. (1956, 256 pp., $4.50).

Logarithmic and Trigonometric Tables, by the Department of Mathematics, U.S. Naval Academy. (Reprinted 1959, 93 pp., $1.65).

Military Law, compiled by Captain J. K. Taussig, Jr., USN and Com-

April 22, 1959

TO THE CORPS OF CADETS, UNITED STATES MILITARY
ACADEMY

I am glad to learn of the forthcoming publication of The West
Point Atlas of American Wars, for use in cadet instruction -- and
indeed for use by all military personnel in the study of military
history.

Through a careful and objective study of the significant campaigns
of the world, a professional officer acquires a knowledge of military experience which he himself could not otherwise accumulate.
The facts of a given battle may no longer serve any practical purpose except as a framework on which to base an analysis; but when
the serious student of the military art delves into the reasons for
the failure of a specific attack -- or soberly analyzes the professional qualities of one of the responsible commanders of the past --
he is, by this very activity, preparing for a day in which he, under
different circumstances, may be facing decisions of vital consequence to his country.

The "principles of war" which this atlas will assist you in studying
are broad.   They apply to air and naval warfare as well as to land
combat.   They are not, in the final analysis, limited to any one
type of warfare, or even limited exclusively to war itself.   But
principles as such can rarely be studied in a vacuum; military
operations are drastically affected by many considerations, one of
the most important of which is the geography of the region.   Thus,
it is important that these campaigns be studied in conjunction with
the very best available in clear and accurate maps.

I am confident that The West Point Atlas of American Wars will
prove a tremendous aid in instructing -- and inspiring -- the minds
of those whose profession it will be to defend the frontiers of the
Free World against all enemies.

Dwight D. Eisenhower

Reproduction of a statement by President Eisenhower used in the
commercial promotion of the copyrighted contents of "The West Point
Atlas of American Wars." Judging by the President's phrasing, the
book is far more of an official work than it is a private one.

mander H. B. Sweitzer, USN. (Revised by Commander M. E. Wolfe, USN, and Lieutenant Commander R. I. Culick, USN, Reprinted 1959, 90 pp., $2.00).

Naval Leadership, prepared at the U.S. Naval Academy for instruction of midshipmen. (1949, 324 pp., $3.00).

Naval Shiphandling, by Commander R. S. Crenshaw, Jr., USN, aided by officers of the Navy, Coast Guard, Merchant Marine and Pilot Service. (1955, 396 pp., $4.50).

Principles of Electronics and Electronic Systems, edited by commander F. S. Quinn, Jr., USN, and John L. Daley, U.S. Naval Academy. (Second edition 1959, 492 pp., $7.50).

Round-Shot to Rockets, by Taylor Peck. A history of the Washington Navy Yard and U.S. Naval Gun Factory. (1949, 267 pp., $3.00).

The Sea War in Korea, by Commander Malcolm W. Cagle, USN, and Commander Frank A. Manson, USN. (1957, 560 pp., $6.00).

The United States Coast Guard, 1790-1915, by Captain Stephen H. Evans, U.S. Coast Guard. A definitive history. (1949, 228 pages, $5.00).

NUCLEAR STUDIES OF THE U.S. ATOMIC ENERGY COMMISSION PUBLISHED BY McGRAW-HILL COMPANY UNDER COPYRIGHT ARRANGEMENTS

Written and edited by scientists who performed research and development work on the atomic energy enterprise under the Manhattan Engineer District and later under the Atomic Energy Commission.

Biological Effects of External Beta Radiation. R. E. Zirkle. The findings of an intensive radio-biological program carried out during World War II at the Clinton Laboratories. (1951, 242 pages, $3.50).

Biological Effects of External Radiation. H. A. Blair. The nature of the biological effects of neutron irradiation. (1954, 508 pages, $7.00).

Biological Effects of External X and Gamma Radiation. R. E. Zirkle. The findings of an intensive radio-biological program carried on during World War II at the National Cancer Institute and elsewhere. (1954, 530 pages, $7.25).

Biological Studies with Polonium, Radium, and Plutonium. R. M. Fink. The distribution and excretion of polonium and radiation, as well as the comparative toxicities of polonium, plutonium, and radium. (1950, 411 pages, $5.50).

11 July 1960

Mr. M. B. Schnapper
Executive Director
Public Affairs Press
419 New Jersey Avenue, S.E.
Washington 3, D. C.

Dear Mr. Schnapper:

Eight pages is quite a bit to quote from a book. Perhaps you would care to tell us what pages in How to Survive on Land and Sea have engaged your interest and how you propose to employ them.

We would appreciate it also if you could let us know the character of Public Affairs Press, an organization with which I, at least, am not familiar.

Sincerely yours,

Frank Uhlig, Jr.
Assistant Editor

The book in question was copyrighted by the U. S. Naval Institute in 1943 and 1951. Its contents are credited: "By Office of Chief of Naval Operations, U. S. Navy". Mr. Uhlig's letter points up the problems that are inevitable in the case of copyrighted material.

HISTORY OF UNITED STATES NAVAL OPERATIONS IN WORLD WAR II

by SAMUEL ELIOT MORISON

In the case of these works it would seem reasonable to assume that they are of a private nature. But why are the royalties payable to the Navy? The merits of the books unquestionably depend substantially on Admiral Morison's skill as writer and historian, but their contents appear to be based primarily on officially acquired information. Did the Admiral prepare the works in his private capacity or as an official Navy historian? Did he receive compensation from the Navy?

CONTENTS

Special permission for republication, either in whole or in part, is not required, *Provided* a credit line is given to the *Recreational Boating Guide*, CG–340, U.S. COAST GUARD, and a statement made that the pamphlet is for sale by the Superintendent of Documents, U.S. Government Printing Office, Washington 25, D.C., at 40 cents a copy.

Extract from a publication issued by the U. S. Coast Guard. The stipulation in the last paragraph is unique in the annals of government publishing. Presumably the Coast Guard feels it can withdraw permission for republication "either in whole or in part" if satisfactory publicity isn't provided. Copyrighting is the logical next step.

CONSTRAINT BY COPYRIGHT

Histopathology of Irradiation from External and Internal Sources. William Bloom. A report of three years of intensive war research undertaken to compare histological changes that result from various types of radiations originating externally and internally. (1948, 808 pages, $10.75).

Industrial Medicine on the Plutonium Project. R. S. Stone. The problems faced at the outset of the Atomic Energy Project in determining the injuries that could result from exposure to radiation, some of the clinical tests devised, and the results of special studies. (1951, 511 pages, $7.00).

Medical Effects of the Atomic Bomb in Japan. A. W. Oughterson and Shields Warren. The results of the investigations by the Joint Commission for the Investigation of the Effects of the Atomic Bomb in Japan following the bombing of Hiroshima and Nagasaki. (1956, 477 pages, $8.00).

Pharmacology and Toxicology of Uranium Compounds (Parts I and II). Carl Voegtlin and H. C. Hodge. Reports comprehensive experimental studies on uranium compounds and includes findings on the toxic action of fluorine and hydrogen fluoride. (1949, 1084 pages, $14.25).

Pharmacology and Toxicology of Uranium Compounds (Parts III and IV). Carl Voegtlin and H. C. Hodge. Research findings concerning chronic inhalation toxicity of uranium compounds and the mechanism of uranium poisoning. (1953, 1379 pages, $18.00).

Toxicology of Uranium. Albert Tannenbaum. Contains reports of investigations on the toxicology of uranium compounds together with associated studies related to uranium pharmacology and toxicology. (1951, 333 pages, $4.75).

The Actinide Elements. G. T. Seaborg, Radiation Laboratory, University of California, and J. J. Katz, Argonne National Laboratory. A comprehensive survey of the chemistry and nuclear properties of the actinide elements. (1954, 870 pages, $11.75).

Analytical Chemistry of the Manhattan Project. C. J. Rodden, New Brunswick Laboratory, Atomic Energy Commission. The analytical chemistry methods used on the Manhattan Project in connection with uranium, thorium, nitrogen, silicon, fluorine, carbon, hydrogen, chlorine, bromine, sulfur, selenium, tellurium, etc. (1950, 748 pages, $10.00).

Bibliography of Research on Heavy Hydrogen Compounds. Alice H. Kimball. (1949, 350 pages, $4.75). Research on heavy hydrogen and its compounds. (1949, 350 pages, $4.75).

The Chemistry and Metallurgy of Miscellaneous Materials: Thermodynamics. L. L. Quill. Research relating to thermodynamics in the

Index
Classified 50-61
Comics 65, 66
EDITORIAL 30
Night Clubs 37
Obituaries 63
Pictures 28, 29
Radio-TV 62, 63
Real Estate 41
Sports 42-49
Theaters 32
Women's 38-40

The ⟨WASHINGTON DAILY⟩ News

37th Year—No. 13   DI. 7-7777   Entered as Second Class Matter at D. C. Post Office

5 CENTS   **FRIDAY, NOVEMBER 22, 1957**

Weather
Cloudy and cool today, high about 50. Cloudy tonight, low 32. Tomorrow, cold. Today at:
9 a. m. 42
10 a. m. 42
11 a. m. 42
12 Noon 44
See Weather Maps on Page 2

GREATER Washington Edition

Air Force Was Given Secret Report About Sputnik 5 Months Ago

U. S. AIR FORCE
PROJECT RAND

RESEARCH MEMORANDUM

A CASEBOOK ON SOVIET ASTRONAUTICS

- F. J. Krieger

RM-1760

21 June 1956

Assigned to _____

This is a working paper. It may be expanded, modified, or withdrawn at any time. The views, conclusions, and recommendations expressed herein do not necessarily reflect the official views or policies of the United States Air Force.

———————— The RAND Corporation ————————
1700 MAIN ST. • SANTA MONICA • CALIFORNIA

At side is the title page of the now-famous report that gave the Air Force advance knowledge about Russia's first Sputnik. Contents of the report were subject to common law copyright held by the Rand Corporation, a public service non-profit enterprise financed by government funds. The headline a b o v e reflected astonishment when contents of the report became known to the press. In the fall of 1958 a book containing the report was published by Public Affairs Press under exclusive advantageous arrangements with the Rand Corporation.

Soviet National Income and Product, 1940-48, by Abram Bergson and Hans Heymann, Jr., 1954
Soviet National Income and Product in 1928, by Oleg Hoeffding, 1954
Labor Productivity in Soviet and American Industry, by Walter Galenson, 1955

The Operational Code of the Politburo, by Nathan Leites, 1951
Air War and Emotional Stress: Psychological Studies of Bombing and Civilian Defense, by Irving L. Janis, 1951
Soviet Attitudes Toward Authority: An Interdisciplinary Approach to Problems of Soviet Character, by Margaret Mead, 1951
Mobilizing Resources for War: The Economic Alternatives, by Tibor Scitovsky, Edward Shaw, Lorie Tarshis, 1951
The Organizational Weapon: A Study of Bolshevik Strategy and Tactics, by Philip Selznick, 1952
Introduction to the Theory of Games, by J. C. C. McKinsey, 1952
Weight-Strength Analysis of Aircraft Structures, by F. R. Shanley, 1952
The Compleat Strategyst: Being a Primer on the Theory of Games of Strategy, by J. D. Williams, 1954
Linear Programming and Economic Analysis, by Robert Dorfman, Paul A. Samuelson, and Robert M. Solow, 1958

Psychosis and Civilization, by Herbert Goldhamer and Andrew W. Marshall, 1949
Soviet Military Doctrine, by Raymond L. Garthoff, 1953
A Study of Bolshevism, by Nathan Leites, 1953
Ritual of Liquidation: The Case of the Moscow Trials, by Nathan Leites and Elsa Bernaut, 1954
Two Studies in Soviet Controls: Communism and the Russian Peasant, and Moscow in Crisis, by Herbert S. Dinerstein and Leon Gouré, 1955
A Million Random Digits with 100,000 Normal Deviates, by the RAND Corporation, 1955

German Rearmament and Atomic War: The Views of German Military and Political Leaders, by Hans Speier, 1957
West German Leadership and Foreign Policy, edited by Hans Speier and W. Phillips Davison, 1957

Approximations for Digital Computers, by Cecil Hastings, Jr., 1955
International Communication and Political Opinion: A Guide to the Literature, by Bruce Lannes Smith and Chitra M. Smith, 1956
Dynamic Programming, by Richard Bellman, 1957

Were any of these Rand studies commissioned by the Air Force or any other official agency? Where did Rand get funds for preparation of the studies? What's justification for their copyrights? "Behind the Sputniks" edited by F. J. Krieger and "The Rise of Khrushchev" by Myron Rush, published by Public Affairs Press and copyrighted by the Rand Corporation, should be in the above list.

broad categories of metallurgy, refractories, and general chemistry. (1950, 329 pages, $4.50).

The Chemistry of Uranium: Part I. The Element, Its Binary and Related Compounds. J. J. Katz, Argonne National Laboratory, and Eugene Rabinowitch. Results of a program of experimental research in uranium chemistry undertaken at the inception of the Atomic Energy Project. (1951, 609 pages, $8.25).

Preparation, Properties, and Technology of Fluorine and Organic Fluoro Compounds. Charles Slesser and S. R. Schram, Atomic Energy Commission. How organic fluoro compounds of various types were prepared and brought to industrial-scale production. (1951, 868 pages, $11.50).

Production of Heavy Water. G. M. Murphy, H. C. Urey, and Isidor Kirshenbaum. A survey of heavy-water plants and their operation; describes the results of pilot-plant studies on development processes. (1955, 394 pages, $5.25).

Radiochemical Studies: The Fission Products. C. D. Coryell. Results of research at Oak Ridge, Los Alamos, and elsewhere. Deals with radioactivity of fission products, radiochemistry, gaseous fission, etc. (1951, 2086 pages, $27.75).

The Transuranium Elements. G. T. Seaborg, Radiation Laboratory; J. J. Katz, Argonne National Laboratory; and W. M. Manning, Argonne National Laboratory. Research on four known transuranium elements: neptunium, plutonium, americium, and curim. Papers concerning radium, actinium, thorium, protactinium, and uranium are also included. (1949, 173 pages, $23.75).

Engineering Developments in the Gaseous Diffusion Process. Manson Benedict and Clarke Williams. Describes research and engineering developments relative to devices necessary in the development of the gaseous diffusion process. (1949, 129 pages, $2.00).

Vacuum Equipment and Techniques. A. Guthrie and R. K. Wakerling. Presents studies and developments of high-vacuum equipment and practice. (1949, 264 pages, $3.75).

Electronics: Experimental Techniques. W. C. Elmore and Matthew Sands. Describes circuits designed for electronic instrumentation at Los Alamos Scientific Laboratory from 1943 to 1945. (1949, 417 pages, $5.50).

Inozation Chambers and Counters. B. B. Rossi and H. H. Staub. The fundamental features of inozation and the general properties of detectors based upon the inozation process. A description is also given of the construction of typical detectors and their operation. (1949, 243 pages, $3.25).

Optical Instrumentation. G. S. Monk and W. H. McCorkle. The principles of design and research in the development of optical glasses to withstand the destructive effects of high-energy radiations, as well as the use of plastic lenses in instruments of high quality and resolution. (1954, 262 pages, $3.75).

Metallurgy of Zirconium. Benjamin Lustman, Atomic Power Division, Westinghouse Electric Corporation, and Frank Kerze, Jr., Reactor Development Division, U.S. Atomic Energy Commission. Zirconium and its application to nuclear reactors, application for other uses, industrial hygiene and safety, etc. (1955, 776 pages, $10.00).

Miscellaneous Physical and Chemical Techniques of the Los Alamos Project: Experimental Techniques. A. C. Graves and D. K. Froman, Los Alamos Scientific Laboratory. A record of developments resulting from experimental work at Los Alamos Scientific Laboratory during World War II. (1952, 323 pages, $3.25).

Spectroscopic Properties of Uranium Compounds. G. H. Dieke and A. B. F. Duncan. Deals with the spectra and preparation of a number of uranium compounds. (1949, 290 pages, $4.25).

The Theory of Isotope Separation as Applied to the Large-Scale Production of U235. Karl Cohen. Covers research done under AEC auspices. Emphasis placed on the general principles and concepts of the separation of uranium isotopes by gaseous diffusion. (1951, 115 pages, $2.50).

Other AEC Studies Published by the McGraw-Hill Company Under Exclusive Arrangements

Chemical Processing and Equipment. Staffs, National Reactor Testing Station and Brookhaven National Laboratory. "Prepared by the Atomic Energy Commission for the First Atoms for Peace Conference in Geneva, 1955." Describes the chemical processing of reactor fuel elements. Deals with enclosures for radioactive operations, decontamination and monitoring instrument arrangements, irradiation facilities, etc. (1955, 302 pages, $6.00).

Reactor Handbook. J. F. Hogerton and R. D. Grass. Vol. I: Reactor physics and radiation shielding. Vol. II: Light- and heavy-water-cooled system, etc. Vol. III: General properties of fuel, moderator, reflector, control, shielding, structural and other materials. (1955, 2475 pages, $37.50).

Reactor Shielding Design Manual. Theodore Rockwell III, Naval Reactors Branch, Atomic Energy Commission. Procedures and data used in designing, constructing, and testing the shielding for naval and Shippingport pressurized water reactors. (1956, 488 pages, $6.00).

THE ARMY AIR FORCES IN WORLD WAR II

The Historical Division of the Army Air Forces has assembled in seven volumes the record of the AAF in World War II.

It has won world-wide acclaim as the definitive history of American air strategy and operations during the war years. With the publication of this seventh and final volume, *Services around the World*, this monumental project is now complete.

Volumes in this series are:

I. PLANS AND EARLY OPERATIONS (January 1939 to August 1942)

II. EUROPE: TORCH TO POINT-BLANK (August 1942 to December 1943)

III. EUROPE: ARGUMENT TO V-E DAY (January 1944 to May 1945)

IV. THE PACIFIC: GUADALCANAL TO SAIPAN (August 1942 to July 1944)

V. THE PACIFIC: MATTERHORN TO NAGASAKI (June 1944 to August 1945)

VI. MEN AND PLANES

VII. SERVICES AROUND THE WORLD

Promotional material about seven volumes "The Historical Division of the Army Air Force has assembled" for publication under private copyright restrictions.

Corrosion and Wear Handbook for Water-Cooled Reactors. D. J. DePaul. Presents data resulting from the development of the Nautilus submarine reactor and the Shippingport Pressurized Water Reactor projects. Originally prepared and processed as TID Report 7006. (1957, 293 pages, $6.00).

NUCLEAR STUDIES OF THE U.S. ATOMIC ENERGY COMMISSION PUBLISHED BY ADDISON-WESLEY PUBLISHING COMPANY UNDER COPYRIGHT ARRANGEMENTS

Radiation Biology and Medicine. W. D. Claus, Division of Biology and Medicine, AEC. A review of advances in research in the uses and effects of nuclear radiation in the life sciences. (1958, 968 pages, $11.50).

Thorium Production Technology. F. L. Cuthbert. Contains practically all the information currently available on thorium production technology. (1958, 320 pages, $6.50).

Project Sherwood—The U.S. Program in Controlled Fusion. Amasa Bishop, European Scientific Representative of A.E.C. Account of the extensive research and development undertaken by the Atomic Energy Commission for harnessing the energy of thermo-nuclear reactions. (1958, 228 pages, $5.75).

Uranium Ore Processing. J. W. Clegg and D. D. Foley. While emphasis is on current practices in the United States, techniques in other countries are also described. Main uranium districts in the U.S. listed. (1958, 448 pages, $7.50).

Boiling Water Reactors. A. W. Kramer. Prepared under the auspices of the Argonne National Laboratory with the cooperation of the scientists and engineers there who conceived and developed this type of reactor. (1958, 592 pages, $8.50).

Fluid Fuel Reactors. J. A. Lane and H. G. MacPherson, Oak Ridge National Laboratory, and Frank Maslan, Brookhaven National Laboratory. Summarizes results of research carried on in the United States for almost ten years. Emphasizes the subject from the chemical standpoint. (1958, 1008 pages, $11.50).

The Shippingport Pressurized Water Reactor. By personnel of the Naval Reactors Branch, Division of Reactor Development, Atomic Energy Commission; and Duquesne Light Company. An account of the

Are these books official or private works? All have been published recently by the D. Van Nostrand Company, Inc.

THE UNITED STATES AIR FORCE REPORT ON THE BALLISTIC MISSILE

Its Technology, Logistics, and Strategy

Edited by Lt. Col. Kenneth F. Gantz

With a Preface by

GENERAL THOMAS D. WHITE, Chief of Staff, USAF

Introduction by MAJOR GENERAL BERNARD A. SCHRIEVER

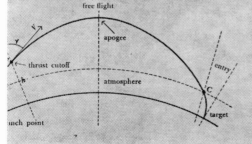

A report by members of the U. S. Air Force on its missile program: its development, its aims, its impact on national policy.

Was this work published by Doubleday under arrangements consistent with the Copyright Law? Note the official seal of the Air Force; ordinarily the seal is not used on non-official works.

research for and development of the first large-scale central station nuclear power plant to be built and operated in the U.S. (1958, 600 pages, $9.50).

Sodium Graphite Reactors. Chauncey Starr and R. W. Dickinson. A presentation of sodium graphite reactor technology. Emphasis is placed on the design and development of the sodium reactor experiment. The Hallam Nuclear Power Facility is described. (1958, 304 pages, $6.50).

Solid Fuel Reactors. J. R. Dietrich and W. H. Zinn. Appraises the technical and economic outlooks for five projected solid fuel nuclear power reactor types. (1958, 864 pages, $10.75).

U.S. Research Reactor Operation and Use. J. W. Chastain, Jr. Sets forth information not only about technical aspects, characteristics, and operating problems but also on administrative, legal, and cost problems. (1958, 384 pages, $7.50).

Physical Metallurgy of Uranium. A. N. Holden. A comprehensive treatment of the physical metallurgy of uranium. Correlates the wealth of information that has become available in the field during recent years. (1958, 272 pages, $5.75).

NUCLEAR STUDIES OF THE U.S. ATOMIC COMMISSION BY D. VAN NOSTRAND COMPANY UNDER COPYRIGHT ARRANGEMENTS

Cryogenic Engineering. R. B. Scott, National Bureau of Standards. Outlines the practical aspects of cryogenic processes and equipment. Prepared by the National Bureau of Standards for the Atomic Energy Commission. (1959, 375 pages, $5.60).

Nuclear Reactor Metallurgy. W. D. Wilkinson and W. F. Murphy, International School of Nuclear Science and Engineering, and W. J. Mc-Gonnagle, Argonne National Laboratory. Production of uranium metal, structure and properties of uranium, mechanical properties of uranium, radiation damage in uranium. Metallurgy of plutonium, thorium, beryllium and zirconium. Course material in applied reactor metallurgy developed at the International School of Nuclear Science and Engineering of Argonne National Laboratory. (1958, $5.60).

Uranium Production Technology. C. D. Harrington and A. E. Ruehle. Presents the entire field of technology in the United States of uranium metal production from uranium concentrates or high-grade uranium ore. Covers work done at official AEC installations throughout this country. (1959, 550 pages, $17.50).

Energy in the Future. P. C. Putnam, Consultant, AEC. An examination of the maximum plausible demands for energy during the next fifty to one hundred years, compared with the ability of nuclear fuels and all non-nuclear sources of energy to meet these demands at low cost. 1953, 556 pages, $12.75).

Sourcebook on Atomic Energy. Samuel Glasstone, Consultant, AEC. A handbook of basic atomic energy information; this is the second edition. Covers properties of nuclear radiations, nuclear transmutations, nuclear forces and nuclear structure, utilization of nuclear energy, uses of isotopes and radiations, and radiation protection and health physics. The first edition went through twelve "large printings." (1958, 641 pages, $4.40).

Nuclear Reactor Experiments. J. B. Hoag, Argonne National Laboratory. Describes 49 experiments involving the theory and practice of fission reactor measurements. (1958, 480 pages, $6.75).

Principles of Nuclear Reactor Engineering. Samuel Glasstone, Consultant, AEC, with the assistance of members of the Oak Ridge National Laboratory staff. The fundamental scientific principles upon which reactor engineering is based. (1955, 861 pages, $7.95).

The Elements of Nuclear Reactor Theory. Samuel Glasstone, Consultant, AEC, and M. C. Edlund, Oak Ridge National Laboratory. The basis of nuclear reactor theory. Nuclear structure and stability. Fission process, diffusion of neutrons, etc. (1952, 416 pages, $4.80).

MISCELLANEOUS NUCLEAR STUDIES OF THE
U.S. ATOMIC ENERGY COMMISSION PUBLISHED
UNDER COPYRIGHT ARRANGEMENTS

Metal Beryllium. D. W. White, Jr., Knolls Atomic Power Laboratory, and J. E. Burke, General Electric Company. Basic information on beryllium. Covers all aspects of beryllium technology emphasizing possible uses of the metal in atomic energy work. (American Society of Metals, 1955, 703 pages, $8.00).

Metal Thorium. H. A. Wilhelm. Detailed information on the fundamental scientific, technological, and engineering aspects of thorium, role of thorium metal in the nuclear field, non-nuclear application of thorium, etc. (American Society for Metals, 1958, 397 pages, $10.00).

Atoms For the World. Laura Fermi, Historian for the official U.S. delegation to the International Conference on the Peaceful Uses of Atomic Energy, Geneva, 1955. An account of the hopes and plans of the U.S. representatives, the problems encountered, the people involved, and the successful culmination of months of planning and work entailed in this country's participation in the Conference. (University of Chicago Press, 1955, 227 pages, $3.75).

RADIATION LABORATORY SERIES PUBLISHED BY McGRAY-HILL UNDER COPYRIGHT ARRANGEMENTS WITH THE U.S. OFFICE OF SCIENTIFIC RESEARCH AND DEVELOPMENT AND THE MASSACHUSETTS INSTITUTE OF TECHNOLOGY

Since the royalties on these books are payable to the U. S. Treasury their contents could well be considered the property of the federal government. To all indications they were commissioned by the U. S. Office of Scientific Research and Development for preparation by experts working under the auspices of the Massachusetts Institute of Technology.

Announced as "one of the most important scientific publishing projects in many years", the series is based upon "the immense developments in electronics and in microwave theory and technique during the war years, which, once secret, have now widely been declassified." Dr. Vannevar Bush, wartime head of the U. S. Office of Scientific Research and Development, was formerly President of the Massachusetts Institute of Technology.

The extensive research that went into the series probably cost the federal government billions of dollars. If the Massachusetts Institute of Technology shared in the cost of preparing the series it certainly would have been entitled to at least a share of the royalties. But it is not inconceivable that all costs were paid by the government.

Radar System Engineering. Louis N. Ridenour. An introduction to the tremendous research and effort that went into the development of radar and related techniques during the war. (748 pages, 1947, $11).

Long Range Navigation. J. A. Pierce, A. A. McKenzie, R. H. Woodward. The design and use of the long-range pulse navigation system known as Loran, both in its original form and as skywave-synchronized Loran. (468 pages, 1948, $8.50).

Radar Beacons. Arthur Roberts . The employment of systems involving beacons for navigation and for identification. (489 pages, 1947, $8.50).

Cathoderay Tube Display. Theodore Soller, Merle A. Starr, George E. Valley, Jr. The basic characteristics, principles of operation, and methods of application of cathode-ray tubes. (746 pages, 1948, $12).

Microwave Magnetrons. George B. Collins. The theoretical and practical aspects of multicavity magnetrons. (769 pages, 1948, $12).

Klystrons and Microwave Triodes. Donald R. Hamilton, Julian K. Knipp,

J. B. Horner Kuper, Brookhaven National Laboratory. Primarily concerned with low-powered microwave triodes and klystrons and their performance as local oscillators, signal generators, and low-powered transmitters. (526 pages, 1948, $10).

Technique of Microwave Measurements. Carol G. Montgomery. A description of technique and apparatus useful to present and future workers in the microwave field; emphasis is on laboratory equipment. 939 pages, 1948, $13.50).

Principles of Microwave Circuits. C. G. Montgomery, R. H. Dicke, E. M. Purcell. A description of guided electromagnetic waves. The results arising from the symmetry properties of microwave junctions are emphasized. (486 pages, 1948, $8.50).

Microwave Transmission Circuits. George L. Ragan. The problems of the transmission of power from one place to another at microwave frequencies. (748 pages, 1948, $11.50).

Microwave Antenna Theory and Design. Samuel Silver. A comprehensive survey of theory and design techniques for microwave antennas, full discussion of antenna measurement methods. (614, pages, 1949, $11).

Microwave Duplexers. L. D. Smullin, C. G. Montgomery. The general problem of using a single antenna for both receiving and transmitting. (430 pages, 1948, $8.50).

Microwave Receivers. S. N. Van Voorhis. A guide to all the elements making up a wide-band receiver. (611 pages, 1943, $10.50).

Components Handbook. John F. Blackburn. Codifies information on the properties and characteristics of electronic components. (624 pages, 1948, $10).

Vacuum Tube Ampliers. George E. Valley, Jr., Henry Wallman. Describes the special constructional techniques pertaining to many different types of amplifier. (744 pages, 1948, $12.50).

Crystal Rectifiers. Henry C. Torrey, Charles A. Whitmer. The theory, properties, manufacture, and use of the silicon and germanium point-contact rectifiers developed for use as microwave converters and for others circuit applications. (434 pages, 1948, $8).

Radar Scanners and Radomes. W. M. Cady, U. S. Naval Ordnance, M. B. Karelitz, General Precision Laboratory, L. A. Turner, Argonne National Laboratory. The problem of mechanical and electrical engineering and of servo design which underlie the design of scanners for practical radar sets. (492 pages, 1948, $9).

Electronic Time Measurements. Britton Chance, R. I. Hulsizer, E. F. MacNichol. A survey of the use of precision timing methods in distance finding; includes detailed designs of precision ranging circuits depending upon both manual and automatic control. (528 pages, 1949, $9.50).

Waveforms. Britton Chance, F. C. Williams, V. W. Hughes, D. Sayre, E.

F. MacNichols, Jr. The generation and use of precisely controlled voltage and currents having varied time dependence and duration. (776 pages, 1949, $12.50).

Pulse Generators. G. N. Glasoe, Jean V. Lebacqz. The theoretical and practical aspects of the generation of power pulses. (728 pages, 1948, $11).

Radar Aids to Navigation. John S. Hall. Describes the advantages and uses of radar equipment when applied to problems of navigation pilotage. (839 pages, 1947, $8.50).

Propagation of Short Radio Waves. D. E. Kerr. Reflections from the earth's surface, radar targets and echoes, etc. (729 pages, 1951, $12.50).

Threshold Signals. J. L. Lawson, G. E. Uhlenbeck. The factors which affect the perception of desired signals in the presence of various kinds of interference. (388 pages, 1950, $8.50).

Waveguide Handbook. N. Marcuvitz. Experimental data on the properties of microwave transmission lines, microwave circuit elements, etc. (428 pages, 1951, $10).

Electronic Instruments. Ivan A. Greenwood, Jr., J. Vance Holdam, Jr., Duncan MacRae, Jr. Treats details of the design of simple electronic computing systems, the practical aspects of the design of lightweight, low-powered electronic servomechanisms. (708 pages, 1948, $12.50).

Computing Mechanisms and Linkages. Antonin Svoboda. Deals with computing mechanisms and linkages, elementary computing mechanisms, Barlinkage computer, basic concepts and terminology. (352 pages, 1948, $8).

RESPONSIBILITIES OF PUBLIC EMPLOYEES

"As a Government employee, you are one of about two and a half million citizens who have been chosen to *serve all the 178 million citizens of the nation.* No private employment carries this distinction, nor does private employment carry the responsibility yours does. You have responsibility both as a private citizen and as a public servant.

"As a public servant you work for everybody in the country—including yourself. If you do a good job, everyone stands to gain. If you work carelessly and indifferently, your lack of productive effort actually drains money from the taxpayers' pockets.

"As a member of the public, you have a personal stake in the Government. How you do your job—effectively or ineffectively—reacts in exactly that way on your own personal interests.

"As an employee in the public service you cannot always do things as you would personally prefer to do them. The laws of the land which express the will of the majority of our citizens, and the rules and regulations under which the laws are carried out, affect your actions.

"Public employees are free to engage in any outside work, either paid or volunteer, provided it is consistent with their responsibilities. A Government employee should not engage in outside work if:

"It will interfere with . . . efficient performance of his official duties.

"His outside employment will be in conflict with the interests of the Federal Government.

"His engaging in the outside employment is a violation of a statute, regulation, or executive order, including state and local statutes and ordinances, as well as federal statutes.

"The outside work may bring criticism or embarrassment to the Government.

"The work takes his time or attention during his official work hours.

"If you engage in outside paid employment . . . report it in writing to your supervisor, describe the work and the amount of time per week you engage in it." (Extracts from "Working Together in the U.S. Civil Service" Civil Service Commission, 1960).

Atomic Energy
for Military Purposes

The Official Report
on the Development of the Atomic Bomb
under the Auspices
of the United States Government,
1940–1945

By HENRY DeWOLF SMYTH

CHAIRMAN, DEPARTMENT OF PHYSICS
PRINCETON UNIVERSITY
CONSULTANT, MANHATTAN DISTRICT, U.S. ENGINEERS

Written at the request of
MAJ. GEN. L. R. GROVES, U.S.A.

PRINCETON

PRINCETON UNIVERSITY PRESS

1 9 4 6

Title page of the historic official report through which the nation first learned details about the development of the atomic bomb. As initially issued and as later reprinted, this work carried the personal copyright of Prof. Smyth. Was the copyright officially ordered? It was possibly used as a precedent for the extensive copyrighting that has been sanctioned and subsidized by the U. S. Atomic Energy Commission. Dr. Smyth was a Commission member from 1949 to 1954.

An advertisement used by D. Van Nostrand Company in promoting the sale of a work which appears to be official in every vital respect.

"He's getting his last minute instructions from *Life*"
(A cartoon by Ed Dahlin in Esquire, July, 1960.)

6

THE RIGHT TO KNOW AND
THE OBLIGATION TO INFORM

Copyrighting of governmental material by government officials is in direct conflict with the First Amendment of the Constitution.

An official holding copyright control over his knowledge of governmental affairs can restrict or prevent anyone from quoting any statement covered by his copyright. This is contrary to the guarantees of the First Amendment. Even the Government of the United States is precluded from using material restricted by private copyright.

The purpose of the First Amendment is to prevent government from restricting in any way the right of the American people to a free and unfettered press. That right becomes meaningless to the extent that government officials can restrain any person or any publication from quoting them or can decide who can or cannot quote them and under what circumstances.

It is the sworn obligation of government officials to uphold the Constitution. Any action by a public servant that diminishes, discourages, or inhibits freedom of press without overwhelming justification in the public interest is in conflict with the oath all public servants take upon assuming office.

At a time when there is much withholding of information from the American people for reasons of national security and executive privilege, the nation can ill afford to countenance copyright restrictions on governmental intelligence for private purposes.

Never in the nation's history has there been a more urgent need for the widest possible dissemination of official information about the activities, policies, and problems of the United States Government. Now that the American way of life is questioned and challenged because Soviet Russia appears to be outstripping us and outsmarting us, it is especially imperative that the American people be fully informed about the vital concerns of government. The United States cannot hope to meet the awesome issues of the nuclear age if its key officials are to be free to carve out for themselves private informational monopolies buttressed by copyright prohibitions.

To permit government officials to restrict what can or cannot be quoted is to encourage return to evils and abuses that existed in the colonies

RADIATION
MONITORING
IN ATOMIC
DEFENSE

This practical working manual for radiological defense personnel provides full details on the use of all standard radiation detectors and the interpretation of their results. It is written for everyone concerned with the measurement of radiation, including civilian, industrial and Armed Services defense workers, and requires no technical background to understand or use.

by DWIGHT E. GRAY

Chief, Navy Research Section, Library of Congress
Formerly Affiliated with Technical Information Service, Atomic Energy Commission

and JOHN H. MARTENS

Technical Information Service, Atomic Energy Commission

Reproduction of jacket copy of another privately copyrighted work.

PRINCIPLES OF NUCLEAR REACTOR ENGINEERING

RADIATION PROTECTION

► Radiation Hazards and Health Physics: Biological Effects of Radiation; Radiation Dose Units; Standards of Biological Protection; Protection of Personnel; Radioactive Waste Disposal; Problems.

SHIELDING OF NUCLEAR REACTOR SYSTEMS

► Reactor Shielding Problems; Shielding Geometry; Shielding of Gamma-Ray Sources; Design of Reactor Shields; Appendix; Problems.

THERMAL ASPECTS OF NUCLEAR REACTOR SYSTEMS

► Thermal Problems in Reactor Design; Design of Cooling System; Heat Sources in Reactor Systems; Heat Transmission by Conduction and Convection; Heat Transmission in Systems with Internal Sources; Temperature Distribution Along Path of Reactor Coolant; Heat Transfer Properties of Fluids; Comparison of Heat-Transfer Properties of Coolants; Pressure Drops and Pumping Power in Coolant Systems; Heat Transfer to Boiling Liquid; Thermal Stresses in Reactor Components; Problems.

NUCLEAR REACTOR DESIGN VARIABLES

► Main Aspects of Reactor Design; Reactor Experiments; Research Reactors; Production Reactors or Converters; Power Reactors; The Nuclear System; Reactor Components; The Heat-Removal System; Preliminary Design Calculations; Economic Aspects of Nuclear Power; Problems.

DESCRIPTIONS OF NUCLEAR REACTORS

► Introduction.

TABLES
INDEX

Extract from a sales promotion circular concerning one of the Atomic Energy Commission documents published by D. Van Nostrand Company under exclusive arrangements.

U.S. SURVEY FINDS OTHERS CONSIDER SOVIET MIGHTIEST

Summer Poll Shows Belief Is Nearly Unanimous Among Nations Sampled

LEAD EXPECTED TO HOLD

Some Expect Gap to Widen —Prestige Issue Fought Over in Campaign

An almost unanimous belief that the Soviet Union is the leading military power was disclosed in a world-wide survey conducted for the United States Government during the summer, reliable sources abroad report.

According to these sources, the survey also disclosed unanimity among the free and uncommitted nations of the world that the Soviet Union would maintain and possibly widen its lead over the United States through the next decade.

These are the major findings of a report drawn up by the Office for Research and Analysis on the basis of the results of the survey. The office is a part of the United States Information Agency.

The survey was made in nine or ten countries, including France, West Germany, Italy, the Netherlands, Belgium, Indonesia, Britain and Pakistan.

Senator J. W. Fulbright presumably had this report in mind when he asserted the Administration was suppressing information that showed a decline in American prestige around the world.

KENNEDY DEMANDS PRESTIGE REPORT

Senator Bids Nixon Release 'Suppressed' U. S. Survey —Campaigns in Michigan

By The Associated Press.
DETROIT, Oct. 26—Senator John F. Kennedy demanded to day that Vice President Nixon have released a secret Government survey report to show that ten nations considered the United States was behind the Soviet Union in military strength.

The Democratic Presidential candidate said the report had been suppressed top rotect Mr. Nixon's assertions that American prestige was at an "all-time high."

He also said that "the present Administration has consistently followed a policy of suppressing important public information."

The White House balked today at making public the report.

Mr. Nixon has said he had no objection to making the report public.

Moves Into Michigan

Senator Kennedy carried his campaign from Illinois into Michigan today.

He said his two days in central Illinois and Chicago suburbs, largely Republican territory in the past, were heartening to him. "I am greatly encouraged by the results here of the chances of carrying Illinois," Mr. Kennedy said.

He put in a heavy day in Michigan, where his chances of winning the state's twenty electoral votes are considered good.

In a speech in Mount Clemens, Senator Kennedy said:

"The present Administration

Continued on Page 26, Column 1

U. S. SURVEY SAYS SUMMIT LOWERED NATION'S STANDING

Secret Document Also Finds a Drop in Soviet Stature in Britain and France

Text of the report appears on Pages 28 and 29.

A "confidential" survey made by the United States Information Agency last June, still kept secret by the Eisenhower Administration, reported that both the United States and the Soviet Union "suffered major losses in general standing with the British and French public" in the wake of the failure of the Paris summit conference.

Copies of the document were obtained by The New York Times yesterday.

The question of United States prestige has become a major issue between Vice President Nixon, the Republican Presidential nominee, and his Democratic rival, Senator John F. Kennedy.

Mr. Kennedy has charged that the nation's prestige is declining. Mr. Nixon has said it is at an "all-time high."

Polled French and British

The report was prepared by the Office of Research and Analysis of the information agency, which polled French and British citizens.

It drew these conclusions:

¶"Though the U. S. S. R. is blamed most for the collapse of the summit conference, a majority blamed both sides at least n part. * * *

¶"Favorable opinion for the United States as a country and

Extracts from the New York Times pointing up the extraordinary situation that confronted the nation in October, 1960, when the White House and the U. S. Information Agency refused to make public a non-confidential report about the nation's diminishing prestige overseas. What was not known at the time was that although the report had been officially commissioned and financed the U. S. Information Agency had granted exclusive publishing rights on its contents to European companies selling information to publishers. Still not known is the extent to which U. S. I . A. is party to private copyrighting of officially prepared material.

U. S. Accused of Allowing Sale Of French Poll Denied Congress

Special to The New York Times.

WASHINGTON, Nov. 4—Representative John E. Moss charged today that the United States Information Agency had permitted a French company to sell its findings on the rating of American prestige abroad while it denied this information to the American Congress.

The California Democrat also said that another foreign company, hired for poll-taking, received exclusive rights to use questions on public opinion that were framed by employes of the U. S. I. A.

Mr. Moss made the charges in a letter to George V. Allen, director of the U. S. I. A. The Representative is chairman of the House special subcommittee investigating the withholding of public information by the Executive Branch of the Government.

Contracts between the agency and private companies for the public opinion polls on America abroad, Mr. Moss contended, run into the dozens. The U. S. I. A., he asserted, has been spending nearly $200,000 a year for such polls, and has given the foreign companies a greater command over the results of the polling than Congress could exert.

Mr. Allen was not in Washington and had not seen Representative Moss' letter. There was no comment from the agency ytyonight.

One issue in the Presidential campaign has been the suppression by the U. S. I. A. of the results of pollings abroad that are said to have indicated that the United States has lost prestige while the Soviet appeared to gain.

Senator J. W. Fulbright, Arkansas Democrat who heads the Senate Foreign Relations Committee, has requested copies of these reports, but they have been withheld. The New York Times has obtained copies of three of the reports and has published them in full text or by lengthy excerpts.

The subcommittee has been provided with "selected" copies of contracts with private companies for the poll-taking, Mr. Moss said. These exhibits, he charged, show that the U. S. I. A.'s contention that the polling results constituted only "staff reports and working papers" and could be withheld under "established policy" of the Executive Brance were invalid.

A New York Times story confirming U. S. Information Agency authorization of private foreign sale of officially commissioned reports. Exclusive right to publish and copyright similar material in the U. S. has also been authorized despite the fact that the Agency is not supposed to be engaged in propaganda activities in this country.

prior to the Revolutionary War. In those days a licensing system strongly reminiscent of present day copyright procedures gave agents of the British Government the right to decide what could be published and, in consequence, what could be read. This is distinctly similar to the situation that exists when modern government officials arrogate to themselves the power to license or not license quotation of statements that should be in the public domain.

If preventive and/or corrective action is not taken government officials will inevitably find it both desirable and advantageous to place copyright restrictions on practically everything of a governmental nature they choose to consider their private property. Unless something is done—and done soon—only the dim witted or truly unselfish public servant will be slow to devise reasons why this or that material should not be set aside for his personal benefit.

As is evident in the origin and development of the statutes affecting copyright, Section 8 of the Copyright Act is not only consonant with the Constitutional guarantees of free speech and press but also a bulwark of those guarantees. In explicitly prohibiting the copyrighting of government publications, this Act protects the American people from bureaucratic abuses of a device never intended for government agencies or their officials as such.

If the phrasing of Section 8 of the Copyright Law means anything it means that it is improper for public officials, high and low, to resort to copyrighting as a means of circumscribing the right of the American people to unhindered access to and use of governmental information.

If, as practically every President of the United States has recognized and as the Supreme Court has repeatedly affirmed, it is the obligation of government agencies and officials to keep the American people informed about the programs, problems and policies of their government then much of the material cited in this report must be considered public property that should be accessible to all via the public domain.

Keeping the American people informed about the policies, activities, and problems of their government is a fundamental responsibility of government officials.

Although there are few statutes that explicitly require the President, members of Congress or public officials in general to keep the nation informed—regularly or otherwise—about the activities, policies, and problems of government, American democracy would be greatly vitiated if they did not recognize and fulfill their implicit obligations in this regard. Keeping the electorate properly advised has long been part of the life blood of the republic.

Of all the various means whereby government can communicate directly and quickly with the American people, none is more effective than the speech which, if not restricted, can be heard in every household, via radio and television, and that can be read, in whole or in part, in the morning or evening newspapers. Compared to this means of government-to-people contact within minutes and hours, every other means of communication has severe limitations.

Nevertheless, a dangerous innovation in the American process of government has been adjudicated into existence by a federal court ruling that public speeches and other prouncements by public officials on public issues (including governmental responsibilities) are their private property and can be placed under copyright restrictions for 28 to 56 years if such prouncements are not "commissioned" by "the United States."[1]

[1] In distinguishing between utterances of a "private" and "official" nature, statements by public officials that relate to governmental responsibilities must be regarded as official. State v. Davis 68 W. Va. 142, 69 S.E. 639, 32 LRA (NS) 501.

That public business on every level of government is the business of the entire public is set forth in voluminous detail in "The People's Right To Know", a report of 405 pages prepared by Harold L. Cross for the American Society of Newsaper Editors and published by Columbia University Press in 1953. A Supplement to this excellent report was published in 1954 by Columbia University Press in 1954 and by the Freedom of Information, University of Missouri, in 1959.

Recent federal government restrictions on information are incisively described by James Russell Wiggins, former President of the American Society of Newspaper Editors, in "Freedom of Secrecy," Oxford University Press, 1956, 242 pages.

For details regarding policies and practices of federal agencies in withholding information from the public see the exhaustive—and almost exhausting—hearings of the Special House Subcommittee on Government Information, popularly known as the Moss Committee because its Chairman, Representative John E. Moss, has since 1955 spear-headed a relentless drive for greater public access to governmental information.

UNITED STATES INFORMATION AGENCY
WASHINGTON

July 21, 1960

Dear Mr. Boskoff:

I refer to previous correspondence from you and your client, Public Affairs Press, regarding publication of the RAMAC material.

As you know, the Agency has made inquiry into the various allegations made by Mr. Schnapper regarding possible unlawful or unethical conduct on the part of Agency employees with respect to the RAMAC materials. As previously advised, the Agency also submitted this matter to the Department of Justice for consideration in accordance with the pertinent provisions of the U. S. Code.

The Department of Justice has concluded its review and we now can advise that the inquiry initiated on the basis of the allegations of your client failed to disclose conduct or acts warranting legal action.

The Agency has ascertained that an arrangement was entered into between two Agency research specialists and the Manhattan Publishing Company for the editing of the RAMAC material. This arrangement was made at the request of the publisher with the full knowledge of their office and all services were rendered off Government premises and outside normal working hours.

The Agency has assured itself that neither these employees nor any other employees of the Agency acted in a manner which improperly placed Public Affairs Press in an unfavorable competitive position as to the RAMAC materials.

Sincerely,

Eugene J. Skora
Assistant General Counsel

Alexander Boskoff, Esquire
1111 E Street, N. W.
Washington, D. C.

The explanation satisfied USIA but will it satisfy Congress or the public? Is it altogether proper for employees of an agency to be party to copyrighting of material commissioned by their own agency? Justice Department never queried Public Affairs Press.

79

4 reasons why we predict this will be one of the best selling books of 1960

Was the advertising copy writer merely indulging in overstatement or was he sticking pretty close to the facts in stating: "It's the first really authentic story of the U. S. Secret Service, taken straight from the files of the Service itself"?   Did Messrs. Bowen and Neal obtain most of their material while in the Secret Service?   Did either of them prepare for official purposes material constituting a substantial portion of their copyrighted book?

7

THE FREE PRESS RIGHTS OF EVERY CITIZEN

Is it consistent with the First Amendment to make freedom of press a commodity that can be apportioned on a discriminatory and piecemeal basis by individual officials at their personal will or whim? This question is posed by every copyright held by a public official on governmental material.

By virtue of his restrictive powers under the Copyright Act an official has it wholly within his power to decide (1) who can quote what he has said, (2) how he can be quoted, (3) when he can be quoted.

Like freedom of speech, freedom of press is fundamentally a right of all the people—a right to a free and unfettered press available to each person, individually and collectively.

Contrary to an erroneous belief, freedom of press is not and never was supposed to be a guarantee established exclusively for those who operate printing presses. Freedom of press is and always has been a right of each American to express himself in print without hindrance by government except in the case of libelous matter, blatant obscenity or incitement to riot.

At the very bedrock of American democracy is the belief that if there is complete freedom of speech and press the common man will be capable of making wise decisions for himself, for his community, and for his nation.

Traditionally, newspapers, magazines and books have been the principal pillars of the press. Each is certainly essential to a well informed America. Newspapers provide the nation with the most up-to-date information about the world in which they live. Magazines offer weekly and monthly enlightenment on the rapidly changing scene. Books fill the gaps left by newspapers and magazines; they provide perspective in depth, informational as well as philosophical.

At the time the Bill of Rights was passed [1] the Founding Fathers had in mind every type of printed publication—periodicals,[2] circulars, pamphlets,

---

[1] To John Milton's eloquent "Areopagitica", foundation stone of true speech and press in the modern world, the Bill of Rights was deeply indebted. The greatest of all of Milton's prose writings, this classic work was evoked by an edict requiring official licensing of pamphlets and books.

Through what appears to have been an oversight Milton had published a treatise on divorce without securing a license through registration in the required manner he had previously observed. This oversight provided an unfriendly government with grounds for filing a complaint against him. Subsequently "Aeropagitica" appeared books, etc. They were well aware that in the years before, during, and after the Revolution handbills, pamphlets and books were the dominant types of publication. Pamphlets were especially important as a highly effective means of crystallizing and unifying public opinion in the momentous events that led to the Revolution and in the trying days when the thirteen colonies fought the greatest military power of the eighteenth century.

In the years after the Revolution—the years in which a new nation took shape with the benefit of truly revolutionary ideas pertaining to freedom of religion, of speech, and of press—pamphlets and books were the chief media of expression regarding the type of governmental institutions the American people desired. It was with full cognizance of such expression that the Founding Fathers came to sense popular dissatisfaction with the Articles of Confederation. And it was with the help of such expressions in the Federalist Papers and myriad pamphlets that the Constitution was formulated, debated, and approved.

By virtue of the First Amendment every citizen has (or should have) the right to print what he thinks, including his views about his government and its officials; the right to criticize them and to quote them. While it is true that relatively few persons exercise this right and that great corporations have come to dominate the press, Congress has not as yet made freedom of the press a special preserve for newspaper publishers.

During the formative years of the Republic it was relatively easy and inexpensive (although by no means simple) for citizens or groups of citizens to undertake the publication of newspapers in order to express their views with continuity. This is no longer the case. Nowadays establishment of even a small weekly requires a substantial outlay of capital. And daily newspapers have become so costly to maintain profitably that their number has been dwindling markedly in recent years.

As a result of this situation pamphlets and books today provide practi-

---

with the subtitle "A Speech of Mr. John Milton For the Liberty of Unlicensed Printing, to the Parliament of England". A devastating attack on the whole system of governmental licensing of the press, the pamphlet dealt a death blow not only to this system, but to all other types of regulation of the press.

Licensing is a major factor in copyrighting. The Copyright Act not only grants the copyright claimant the right to license as he sees fit, but it also permits him to prevent the public as well as the press from quoting what he has copyrighted.

[2] Not until 1784 did the struggling republic have a daily newspaper—The Pennsylvania Packet and Daily Advertiser, a four page publication devoted chiefly to local shipping and commercial news. At the outbreak of the Revolution there were 35 periodicals in all of the Colonies. Localized in content, interest, and circulation, most were weeklies and monthlies that devoted far more of their space to topical themes, chiefly through letters and essays, than to news as such.

Cannon's Procedure *in the* House of Representatives

By Clarence Cannon

Member of Congress; sometime Parliamentarian of the House,
Speaker pro tempore, Chairman of the Committee of the
Whole; Chairman of Committee on Appropriations, Etc.

with notes and addenda

by

William T. Roy

Kenneth Sprankle   Paul M. Wilson

UNITED STATES GOVERNMENT PRINTING OFFICE, WASHINGTON 25, D. C., 1959

Ripley wouldn't believe it but it's under private copyright—Representative Cannon's. It may be contrary to the First Amendment but it has the blessing of both chambers of Congress.

JOINT RESOLUTION, APPROVED MAY 4, 1959

Resolved by the Senate and House of Representatives of the United States of America in Congress assembled, That there shall be printed and bound for the use of the House one thousand five hundred copies of Cannon's Procedure in the House of Representatives, by Clarence Cannon, to be printed under the supervision of the author and to be distributed to the Members by the Speaker.

SEC. 2. That, notwithstanding any provision of the copyright laws and regulations with respect to publications in the public domain, Cannon's Procedure in the House of Representatives shall be subject to copyright by the author thereof.

Public Law 122—86th Congress

Copyright, 1959
by
Clarence Cannon

The above appears directly after the title page of "Cannon's Procedure in the House of Representatives". Copyrights on earlier versions of the work as printed by the Government Printing Office were previously approved by Congress. However, existence of the copyrights has not been noticed by the public at large.

SENATE PROCEDURE

Precedents and Practices

BY

CHARLES L. WATKINS, *Parliamentarian*

AND

FLOYD M. RIDDICK, *Assistant Parliamentarian*

UNITED STATES SENATE

Although it's the bible of official procedure of the nation's highest legislative chamber it's the private property of Copyright Registrants Charles L. Watkins and Floyd M. Riddick. Very much to their advantage was the precedent set when Congress permitted Rep. Cannon to copyright the procedural handbook of the lower chamber. Were members of the 84th Congress fully aware of the implications involved when they authorized the Watkins-Riddick copyright on May 2, 1958?

cally the only means left for the average citizen to express himself via the printed word. Fortunately it is still possible and feasible for any American who has something to say to become his own pubisher simply by engaging the services of a printer for the publication of a leaflet, pamphlet or book expressing his ideas upon any subject under the sun. Fortunately, too, it is still possible for a small businessman to become a book publisher; here is one of the very few areas left where independence of spirit can be expressed without the benefit of great wealth.

However, if freedom of press is to be reserved solely for news periodicals —as preferred by copyrighting officials who welcome the benefits of newspaper publicity but object to quotation by other press media or by the public at large—then the individual citizen who wants to print what he thinks and the book publisher who is willing to publish what others think should perhaps be designated as second class citizens and deprived of their Constitutional rights. Whatever the disadvantages of such action, it would at least put a realistic end to a popular illusion still harbored by many. This might not please the Founding Fathers if they were around, but it's just possible that they would be sensible enough to recognize that governmental copyrighting is pointless if the fruits of freedom of press are to be fully enjoyed by every citizen.

Without free speech, free press can, of course, be drastically curtailed— and vice versa. It is because of their very close interrelationship that they are referred to in almost the same breath—"freedom of speech or of the press"—in the Bill of Rights. Admiral Rickover himself could not have been unmindful of their close interrelationship when he declared in one of his copyrighted speeches: "The importance of free speech in a democracy cannot be over-stated. It is a privilege which may be lost if it is not used . . . it is a necessity for insuring good government." Yet, ironically enough, these very words were trussed up by the Admiral's copyrights.

Admiral Rickover is, of course, right when he says that "free speech in a democracy is a privilege which may be lost if it is not used." But how long can free speech be meaningful if these very words could not be quoted except by special permission of a copyrighting official?

In the very same copyrighted speech, Admiral Rickover stated: "Public debates on national issues are an important part of the democratic process. Through them the citizen is enabled to familiarize himself with facts which he might not have had the time or ability to dig up for himself. By hearing opposing 'experts' give their interpretations of these facts and their solutions to the problem under discussion, the citizen discovers all aspects of the issue and is helped to make wise decisions." How can truly wise decisions be reached by the American people if such statements by a public servant are under copyright restrictions?

85th Congress ⎱
2d Session ⎰

COMMITTEE PRINT

SPACE HANDBOOK:
ASTRONAUTICS AND ITS APPLICATIONS

STAFF REPORT
OF THE
SELECT COMMITTEE
ON
ASTRONAUTICS AND SPACE EXPLORATION

UNITED STATES
GOVERNMENT PRINTING OFFICE
WASHINGTON : 1959

23400

Its contents are subject to copyright restrictions. How come is difficult to explain. Some ingenious lawyers deserve all the credit—or blame. To all indications its contents were officially "commissioned . . . [by] the United States".

Beresford Copyrights His Speech

United Press International

The special counsel of the House Space Committee, following a precedent set by Vice Adm. Hyman G. Rickover, has copyrighted a speech he will make at an international meeting next Tuesday.

Spencer M. Beresford said Rickover's action influenced him to copyright his speech to the International Astronautical Federation at Stockholm, Sweden.

The Space Committee distributed advance copies of the speech in the House press gallery this week, along with a noncopyrighted summary.

Beresford said he copyrighted the speech because parts of a noncopyrighted address he made last year were published in a professional journal with little attribution. He said the press would be permitted to quote from his Stockholm speech with attribution.

Rickover, so-called father of the nuclear submarine, won a court suit last year challenging his right to copyright his speeches on education.

Who commissioned Mr. Beresford to go to Amsterdam to deliver his copyrighted speech? Who paid his travel expenses? Did he deliver his speech in his personal capacity?

6

FREEDOM OF PRESS IS INDIVISIBLE

Since copyright officials and agencies — meaning officials and agencies with a proclivity for copyrighting officially derived material — tend to be fairly sophisticated and realistic about what they want, they have little or no cause to object if their copyrights are ignored by newspapers and news magazines. Indeed, they usually welcome quotation by the New York Times, the Christian Science Monitor, Time, Newsweek, etc. Such publicity is excellent grist for bureaucratic publicity mills.

Where's the harm, then, if a Rickover copyrights his public speeches but permits news publications to quote them? Seemingly none, but plenty is fundamentally askew.

Every editor who accepts the stated or implied terms laid down by a copyrighting official automatically gives those terms a validity which can some day be used to the disadvantage of his publication and, inevitably, to the detriment of free speech and press for the country at large.

The editor who uses copyrighted material via acceptance of *permission* to quote it provides the copyright claimant with proof positive that his property rights are recognized by the press. Once this has taken place the copyright claimant can, if he wishes, withdraw permission, insist upon payment or stipulate such publicity conditions as he finds desirable. The editor who accepted the validity of his copyright in the first place is morally and legally in a weak position to reject them in the second place.

Freedom of press that depends upon permission, implied or stated, is nothing more than freedom of press by leave of the copyright claimant. This is akin to the freedom an imprisoned man enjoys when his jailer lets him take a walk in the prison yard because he has agreed to walk backwards instead of forward.

Freedom of press by sufferance,[1] by dependence on the capricious will or

[1] In an editorial regarding the Rickover copyrights the San Jose (Calif.) Mercury commented:

"The fact that Admiral Rickover appended the note, 'no permission needed for press use,' does not mitigate the danger inherent in this situation. The fact remains that the public, through its free press, was granted access to Admiral Rickover's remarks only at the admiral's sufferance and not as a matter of right.

"It follows obviously that if a public official can copyright his public speeches he has at his disposal a weapon which can be used to thwart the people's right to know what their officials are doing and saying. This, we believe, is not in the public interest."

Mira temporum felicitas ubi sentiri quæ velis, & quæ sentias dicere licit.

Tacit.

THE Liberty of the Preſs is a Subjeᘏt of the greateſt Importance, and in which every Individual is as much concern'd as he is in any other Part of Liberty: Therefore it will not be improper to communicate to the Publick the Sentiments of a late excellent Writer upon this Point, ſuch is the Elegance and Perſpicuity of his Writings, ſuch the inimitable Force of his Reaſoning, that it will be difficult to ſay any Thing new that he has not ſaid, or not to ſay that much worſe which he has ſaid.

There are two Sorts of Monarchies, an abſolute and a limited one. In the firſt, the Liberty of the Preſs can never be maintained, it is inconſiſtent with it; for what abſolute Monarch would ſuffer any Subjeᘏt to animadvert

Opening words of Peter Zenger's historic advocacy of freedom of the press as "a Subject of the greatest Importance . . . in which every Individual is as much concerned as he is in any other Part of Liberty". Contrary to popular belief, freedom of press is not a right designed for a particular industry or segment of an industry. Freedom of press, including freedom from copyright restrictions on official material, is an inalienable right of every citizen.

whim of copyrighting officials, is wholly contrary to the First Amendment. Freedom of press isn't something that public officials should be permitted to apportion on a discriminatory basis.

It was on the theory that he was free to decide how his speeches could be quoted and by whom, Admiral Rickover appended the following statements to two of his copyrighted speeches: "No permission needed for contemporaneous press use. Above copyright notice to be used if most of speech reprinted." To this stipulation vigorous objection was expressed by V. M. Newton as Chairman of the Freedom of Information Committee of Sigma Delta Chi, the nation's leading journalistic society. In a blunt letter to the Admiral, Mr. Newton stated:

"It is with great concern that we view your action in copyrighting your public speeches and we fear also that this is a deliberate move on your part to limit future publication of your thinking, and particularly so when you perhaps should undergo criticism from the taxpayers.

"I realize that your copyright permits contemporaneous press use of your speeches, but it does not permit use of them or any part of them say a month after they were delivered. This, of course, cuts off use of them in public criticism after say a month's reflection by the tax-paying citizen. It also restricts communication of your views to a narrow section of the free American press and limits their publication to hurried news accounts prepared against deadlines.

"You, as an admiral in the U.S. Navy, are a public servant, answerable to the tax-paying citizens who employ you. And I have the strong belief that all of your actions and particularly all of your public statements, all made from your position as a prominent public servant, should have the widest possible communication among all American taxpayers." (Letter dated April 24, 1959.)

Still harboring the notion that freedom of press was subject to his personal preferences, Admiral Rickover informed Mr. Newton on May 6, 1959:

"It did not occur to me that there would be any newspaper interest in using the material after a few days had passed and if there should be I shall promptly authorize such use. However, in the light of your suggestion I am going to change the expression in future cases by deleting the word 'contemporaneous' and making it clear that newspapers and news periodicals are free to use the material without any limitation as to time . . ."

In short, the Admiral admitted it was his original view that his "contemporaneous" stipulation meant that his speeches could not be quoted "a few days" after they had been delivered and that the "press" meant merely publications of the type he considered acceptable.

At the present time the phrasing of the Admiral's copyright notice is as follows: "No permission needed for newspaper or news periodical use." All other segments of the press please note.

FREEDOM OF PRESS PRINCIPLES

"Our liberty depends on the freedom of the press, and that cannot be limited without being lost."—*Thomas Jefferson*

"The freedom of the press is one of the great bulwarks of liberty and can never be restrained but by despotic governments."—*George Mason*

"Freedom of conscience, of education, of speech, of assembly are among the very fundamentals of democracy and all of them would be nullified should freedom of press ever be successfully challenged."—*Franklin D. Roosevelt*

"A free press maintains the Majesty of the People."—*John Adams*

"Freedom of the press is the staff of life for any vital democracy."—*Wendell L. Wilkie*

" 'We the People' no longer have to beg for rights . . . This is the philosophy behind the command of the First Amendment."—*Justice William O. Douglas*

"A strong society of free men must be kept fully informed . . . When Americans know the truth, they are strong and free to act for the best interest of the Nation and the world."—*President Eisenhower*

"Liberty of the press is essential to freedom in the state. It ought not to be restricted in this commonwealth."—*Constitution of Massachusetts*

"The entire and absolute freedom of the press is essential to the preservation of government on the basis of a free constitution."—*Daniel Webster*

"Knowledge will forever govern ignorance. And a people who mean to be their own governors must arm themselves with the power knowledge gives. A popular government without popular information or the means of acquiring it is but a prologue to a farce or a tragedy, or perhaps both."—*James Madison*

"The liberty of the press is indeed essential to the nature of a free state . . . this consists of laying no previous restraints upon publications . . . "—*William Blackstone*

"The press shall be free to every citizen who undertakes to examine the official conduct of men acting in a public capacity."—*Constitution of Delaware*

"Without the knowledge of what is done by their representatives, in the use of the powers entrusted to them, the people cannot profit by the power of choosing them, and the advantages of good government are unattainable."—*James Mill*

"A free press stands as one of the great interpreters between the government and the people. To allow it to be fettered is to fetter ourselves."—*The Supreme Court (Grosjean vs. the American Press Co., 1936)*

"The liberty of the press is not confined to newspapers and periodicals. It necessarily embraces pamphlets and leaflets. These indeed have been historic weapons in the defense of liberty, as the pamphlets of Thomas Paine and others in our own history abundantly attest."—*The Supreme Court (Lovell vs. City of Griffin, 1938)*

If public officials who follow Admiral Rickover's example are free to do as they choose they are, of course, then free to restrict quotation of their "private" speeches (or other pronouncements) by radio stations, television broadcasters, weekly periodicals of opinion, monthlies and quarterlies, book publishers of every type, historians who write articles and/or books, and, of course, every American citizen.

As long as public officials are to copyright as they choose they can do as they choose. Tomorrow they can, if they see fit, apply their copyright restrictions to particular types of newspapers, or, if they wish, to newspapers with editorial policies they consider unsatisfactory. Who is to say them nay if they are adjudicated "free agents" rather than public officials?

The Founding Fathers did not, of course, establish freedom of press solely for a particular segment of the press. Although the Atlantic Monthly, the Yale Quarterly, and the Harvard Law Review do not happen to have 11 pica columns, they are certainly as much a part of the nation's press as the St. Louis Post-Dispatch and the Kansas City Star. The publications of trade unions and business associations may not be to everyone's liking but they are clearly entitled to the same basic rights as Time and Newsweek.

It has long been established that all types of printed matter—newspapers, magazines, books, pamphlets, leaflets, etc.—are covered by the guarantees of the First Amendment. This is plainly evident in all of the rulings of the Supreme Court and it is especially clear in the more rceent decisions of the Court.

In 1939 the Supreme Court held in Schneider v. Town of Irvington: "This court has characterized the freedom of speech and that of the press as fundamental personal rights and liberties. This phrase is not an empty one and was not lightly used. It reflects the belief of the framers of the Constitution that exercise of the rights lies at the foundation of free government by free men. It stresses, as do many opinions of this court, the importance of preventing the restriction of enjoyment of these liberties.[3]

In 1952 the Supreme Court declared in the Burstyn v. Wilson case: "That books, newspapers and magazines are published and sold for profit does not prevent them from taking a form of expression whose liberty is safeguarded by the First Amendment."[4]

And in 1957 the Court held in Roth v. United States: "All ideas having even the slightest redeeming social importance . . . have the full protection of the guaranties, unless excludable because they encroach upon the limited area of more important interests."[5]

[2] 303 U.S. 444, 452.
[3] 308, U.S. 147.
[4] 343 U.S. 495, 501.
[5] 354 U.S. 476, 484.

APPRAISALS OF PUBLIC AFFAIRS PRESS

Views Expressed Since Its Establishment in 1938

"Your organization is geared to render a very useful public service."—*Joseph H. Willits, Director of the Social Sciences, Rockefeller Foundation.*

"At a time when the need for informed and constructive thought is great your organization is rendering an invaluable service in fostering such thought. I am glad to be able to offer congratulations on the occasion of your fifth anniversary."—*Frank Murphy, Associate Justice of the Supreme Court.*

"It has been refreshing to watch . . . your honest and impartial operations. I have every confidence your work will expand in importance."—*Elmer Davis.*

"Your organization is certainly making a splendid contribution to the fund of human knowledge. Its publications have unquestionably yielded an important influence on the understanding of public affairs."—*Paul Douglass, President, American University.*

"I have followed your work with great interest and am free to say that I know of no other organization of its kind which has ever succeeded in doing so effective a piece of work in the publication and distribution of pamphlet effective a piece of work in the publication and distribution of pamphlet literature."—*James Shotwell, President, Carnegie Endowment International Peace.*

"Public Affairs Press has shown an alertness and awareness as to what has been needed . . . I wish that more civilian organizations had the heartfelt interest of national defense that you have shown."—*Col. Joseph Greene, Editor of the Infantry Journal.*

"In bringing vital materials, pamphlets and books within reach of all sorts of organizations and groups, it is more needed now than ever."—*Chester S. Williams, Director of Adult and Civic Education, U. S. Office of Education.*

"I think you are making an important contribution to the public understanding of world affairs."—*Quincy Wright, Professor of International Law, University of Chicago.*

"May I congratulate you on the great job you are doing."—*Peter Odegard, President, Reed College.*

"Let me congratulate you on the excellent publications you have brought into existence."—*Kenneth Colegrove, Secretary, American Political Science Ass'n.*

"Today one of the most convincing signs of the vitality of our democracy is the revival of the discussion method. One of the most important reasons for this revival of interest is the outstanding work being done by public spirited organizations such as yours in providing material for discussion."—*M. L. Wilson, Director of Extension Work, U. S. Department of Agriculture.*

In his opinion in connection with the case of United States v. Powe, Judge Sibley of the Fifth Circuit Court of Appeals emphasized the particular importance of freedom from restraint in connection with the publication of material relating to government: "Because the federal government is a republican one in which the will of the people ought to prevail, and because that will ought to be expressive of an informed public opinion, the freedom of speaking and printing on subjects relating to that government, its elections, its laws, its operations and its officers is vital to it." [6]

Of all the decisions of the Supreme Court of the United States on matters of a directly pertinent nature none is more important than the ruling of the Court in 1938 in the Lovell v. City of Griffin case. In this case, a case decided on the basis of freedom of press considerations much further removed than in situations involving copyrighting by government officials, a unanimous Court held:

"The struggle for the freedom of the press was primarily directed against the power of the licensor. . . . And the liberty of the press became initially a right to publish *without* a license what formerly could be published only *with* one.' While this freedom from previous restraint upon publication cannot be regarded as exhausting the guaranty of liberty, the prevention of that restraint was a leading purpose in the adoption of the constitutional provision. . . .

"The liberty of the press is not confined to newspaper and periodicals. It necessarily embraces pamphlets and leaflets. These indeed have been historic weapons in the defense of liberty, as the pamphlets of Thomas Paine and others in our own history abundantly attest. The press in its historic connotation comprehends every sort of publication which affords a vehicle of information and opinion. . . . " [7]

Licensing is a major factor in copyrighting. The Copyright Act not only grants the copyright owner the right to license as he sees fit but also permits him to prevent the press as well as the public from quoting what he has copyrighted.

---

[6] Cited in "Federal Protection of Civil Rights," by R. K. Carr, p. 103.

[7] Cited in "Free Speech in the United States," Zechariah Chafee, Jr., p. 403.

TYPICAL PUBLIC AFFAIRS PRESS PUBLICATIONS

Freedom of Speech by Radio and Television. By Elmer E. Smead. A study of government regulation of programs, procedures, conflicts, industry problems, etc. Introduction by Morris Ernst.

In Defense of Democracy. By Frank Murphy. A pamphlet based upon speeches by a distinguished member of the Supreme Court. Foreword by Charles Beard.

Liberty and Learning. By D. Edison Bunting. An authoritative account of the efforts of the American Civil Liberties Union in behalf of freedom of speech and thought in the school.

Liberty Concepts in Labor Relations. By Byron Abernathy. An appraisal of the ideas and ideals of employers and trade unions. Introduction by Roger Baldwin.

Our Human Rights. By Rebecca Chalmers Barton. The experiences of the Wisconsin Commission on Human Rights. Introduction by Governor Walter J. Kohler.

National Defense. By Franklin D. Roosevelt. Basic principles set forth in notable speeches by one of the nation's greatest Presidents.

Freedom of Assembly and Anti-Democratic Groups. A stirring memorandum prepared by the Council for Democracy and published with its cooperation.

Forerunners of Freedom. By Jerome Nathanson. An appraisal of the contributions made by John Dewey, William James, Walt Whitman, and Emerson.

America's Struggle for Free Schools. By Sidney Jackson. A history of the rise of the public school system and its relationship to American democracy.

Democracy by Discussion. By Emory Bogardus. Stimulating ideas by a leading American educator.

Journalism in Wartime. Edited by Frank Mott. A symposium by Palmer Hoyt, Byron Price, Kent Cooper, Erwin Canham and others.

Information and Censorship. By Elmer Davis and Byron Price. A review of wartime problems in speeches by administrators of the Office of War Information and the Office of Censorship.

Fifth Column Lessons for America. By Col. William Donovan and Edgar Mowrer. A pamphlet version of official information of vital concern to every American.

Organized Anti-Semitism in America. By Dr. Donald S. Strong. A scholarly study based upon information obtained from government sources.

Treason: Disloyalty and Betrayal in American History. By Nathaniel Weyl. A comprehensive history of efforts to undermine American democracy.

The Truth About Communism. By Dorothy Thompson. A pamphlet about the antithesis of American principles.

Prejudice and Property. By Tom Clark and Philip Perlman. An indictment of racial discrimination as perpetuated by restrictive property covenants. Based upon a Justice Department brief to the Supreme Court.

Wilson's Ideals. A collection of extracts from speeches on democracy by a notable President.

FARMERS
AND
DEFENSE

By Claude R. Wickard
Secretary of Agriculture

Public Affairs Press, Washington, D. C.

In Defense
of
Democracy

by FRANK MURPHY

Introductory Notes

CHARLES A. BEARD
FRANKLIN D. ROOSEVELT

American Council on Public Affairs

These pamphlet reprints of speech and other material by high public officials helped inform the nation about governmental responsibilities. Their publication by Public Affairs Press, commended as a public service, would not have been possible had the original matter been copyrighted as in the case cited in this report. Contents of the pamphlets were not copyrighted or otherwise subject to restriction.

PREJUDICE AND PROPERTY

An Historic Brief Against Racial Covenants

SUBMITTED TO THE SUPREME COURT

By TOM C. CLARK
Attorney General of the U. S.

AND

PHILIP B. PERLMAN
Solicitor General of the U. S.

PUBLIC AFFAIRS PRESS
WASHINGTON, D. C.

Fifth Column Lessons for America

By Col. WILLIAM DONOVAN
and
EDGAR MOWRER

Introduction
By FRANK KNOX
Secretary of the Navy

American Council On Public Affairs
WASHINGTON, D. C.

9

HOW GOVERNMENTAL COPYRIGHTING
CAME TO BE PROHIBITED BY LAW

Mindful of the nation's deeply rooted antipathy toward bureaucratic restriction of freedom of speech and press, government officers have traditionally been so respectful of the guarantees of the Bill of Rights that, prior to 1895, it was a generally recognized but unwritten law that copyrighting of governmental material by government officials (or by anyone else for that matter) was completely beyond the pale. There was no statute on the subject because none was necessary.

Between the founding of the Republic and 1895, when statutory prohibition was first enacted, instances of copyrighting by public officials were so few and far between that no bills on the subject were proposed in Congress. In the relatively few relevant legal cases that arose in this period, none necessitated a court decision dealing with the question of whether a federal agency could copyright material of an official nature. Moreover, the courts made short shrift of even peripheral efforts to place copyright restrictions on material of an official nature.

In Heine v. Appleton, the first important case of a pertinent nature, a federal court held in 1857 that an employee of the federal government could not claim copyright in material prepared by him in the course of his official work even though his duties did not require him to prepare the material he sought to copyright.[1]

This case involved pictures depicting Commodore Perry's historic expedition to Japan in 1853, drawn by a member of the expedition in what he insisted was his private capacity. Although cognizant that the official duties of the copyright claimant did not require him to draw any pictures of the expedition, the court considered this immaterial in the light of the undisputed fact that he did his drawings while in the government service and that their subject matter was of an official nature. Moreover, the court considered the drawings public property because they had been "given to the public" in an officially printed publication.

In Banks v. Manchester, a very peripheral case that arose in 1888, the court indicated that if a government agency had made a copyright claim it would have been invalidated.[2]

[1] 11 Fed. Cas. 1031, 6324 C.C.S. New York, 1857.
[2] 128 U.S. 244, 1888.

December 21, 1939

Dear Mr. Schnapper:

I am glad to learn of your plans to launch an educational program in which emphasis will be laid on the vital necessity for maintaining our civil liberties.

Those priceless rights, guaranteed under the Constitution, have been the source of our happiness from our very beginnings as a nation. We have been accustomed to take them as a matter of course. Now, however, when we see other nations challenging those liberties, it behooves us to exercise that eternal vigilance which now, as always, is the price of liberty No matter what comes we must preserve our national birthright: liberty of conscience and of education, of the press and of free assembly, and equal justice to all under the law.

As a free people we must defend our dearly won heritage of freedom against all assaults. I wish your organization Godspeed in its work.

Very sincerely yours,

Franklin D Roosevelt

Mr. M. B. Schnapper,
Executive Secretary,
American Council on Public Affairs,
1721 Eye Street,
Washington, D. C.

A letter from President Roosevelt commending the editor of Public Affairs Press for efforts he spear-headed in behalf of freedom of press and other civil liberties. These efforts have included publication of non-copyrighted pamphlets containing speeches by public officials on the basic principles of American democracy.

CONSTRAINT BY COPYRIGHT

Not until the beginning of the present century did it become necessary for Congress to enact statutory prohibition of copyrighting of material of an official nature. Significantly, this action was taken by Congress for the express purpose of preventing copyrighting by one of its own members. Moreover—and also quite significantly—the statute thus enacted arose out of circumstances surprisingly similar to those in the Rickover case: copyrighting of officially delivered addresses. When bit by bit the circumstances became fully known to the nation it became plainly evident that copyrighting by public servants of material of an official nature was considered highly improper.

L'affaire Richardson is a truly extraordinary episode in the history of Congress. It came to a strange climax when, to the astonishment of the public and the press, a compilation of Presidential addresses (including Washington's Farewell Address and Lincoln's Gettysburg Address[3]) was published by Rep. James D. Richardson under his personal copyrights with plates manufactured at public expense. Entitled "The Messages and Papers of the Presidents", the work was published for the Congressman by "The Bureau of National Literature".

How Richardson's unique publishing venture came into being and how he persuaded himself that it should be placed under personal copyright restrictions is a truly fascinating story.[4] In the light of this story and subsequent action taken by Congress it is difficult to believe that public officials can place valid copyrights on works of a predominantly official nature.

By way of justifying the copyright restrictions he had placed on the speeches of the Presidents, Rep. Richards sporadically offered a series of explanations not unlike those made by modern day bureaucrats with copyrighting proclivities.

First of all, Rep. Richardson contended, his duties as a Congressman did not require him to compile the material he assembled and copyrighted. Second of all, his task was self-designated and his services were entirely voluntary. Thirdly, he had devoted to the project a considerable amount of unspecified time he considered his own.

Ostensibly speaking in both his private and personal capacity, the Congressman insisted there was no harm in what he had done since he had decided not to claim copyright as against the government.

[3] Since these pronouncements were not legally required by the official responsibilities of the Presidents, they could be subject to private copyright under the decisions of the courts in the Rickover case. See details on pages 141-147 of the present work.

[4] The whole complex story cannot be told here. Its details are fully recorded in the volumes of the Congressional Record of 1897 and a special Senate report released in 1900.

Did Rep. Richardson claim copyright as against the public? Yes, but it was hardly his intention to prevent quotation of particular Presidential speeches.

Did not his copyright notices automatically circumscribe quotation of the Presidents' speeches by the public? True they might have that effect but he was hardly to blame for that. It was not his fault that the Copyright Law did not require (and still does not require) copyright notices to be explicit as to what is covered by copyright restriction.

At minimum, Rep. Richardson insisted, his copyrights were justifiable because he could claim a property right in the form of his publication and in the indexes prepared for the work. Whether, however, the form was a product of his personal "creativity", whether the indexes were prepared with the assistance of members of his official staff, whether the facilities he had used were public or private—all these things remained unclear, intentionally or otherwise.

How did Rep. Richardson secure printing plates made at public expense? That was surprisingly easy. In his role as Chairman of the Joint Committee on Printing he had obtained authorization whereby the plates were manufactured and furnished to him by the Government Printing Office. By his own say so he was fully entitled to the plates because his compilation of the President's speeches was a public service for which he had not been compensated. True he had been offered official remuneration for the work he had done but that was immaterial since he had declined such remuneration. Judging by the fact that his use of the plates enabled him to earn royalties amounting to $11,320, the Congressman must have had more than a premonition as to why he should pass up more modest official remuneration.

To some persons Rep. Richardson's explanations seemed plausible and satisfactory, but the general consensus was that his copyrights set a dangerous precedent. Putting aside amenities, several legislators reacted to his picadillos with a bluntness that must have affected the coloring in his face, particularly when the suggestion was made that he was less than patriotic in putting copyrights on the holy writ of Presidential messages. More restrained colleagues firmly put him in his place on technical grounds, insisting that he had clothed his acts with official status and that the material at issue was public, not private, property.

To make matters worse for Mr. Richardson, but somewhat better for an embarrassed House of Representatives that felt it had been let down by one of its own, an investigation was ordered by the Senate. Carefully eschewing the questionable nature of Rep. Richardson's conduct, a Senate committee issued a report in which it held that Section 52 of the Printing Act of 1895 precluded and invalidated Rep. Richardson's copyrights. Still in force, this Act provides "That no publication reprinted from . . . stereotype or electrotype plates [made at Government expense] and no other Government publication shall be copyrighted."

The Senate report was unequivocal:

". . . the prohibition contained in the Printing Act was intended to cover every publication authorized by Congress in all possible forms . . .

"Your committee thinks that copyright should not have issued in behalf of the Messages, and that *the law as it stands is sufficient to deny copyright to any and every work once issued as a government publication.* If the services of any author or compiler employed by the Government require him to be compensated, payment should be made in money, frankly and properly appropriated for that purpose, and *the resulting book or other publication in whole and as to any part should be always at the free use of the people, and this, without doubt, was what Congress intended."* [5]

Considered in the light of the Senate judgment in the Richardson case, it is doubtful in the extreme that any but a small number of the copyrights cited herein are either proper or valid.

To all indications the strong phrasing of the Senate report and the general scandal surrounding the copyright incident cost Rep. Richardson the chance of being chosen Speaker of the House of Representatives. A Tennessean who had risen high in Democratic councils, he lost both ground and prestige in subsequent years.

However, it is to Rep. Richardson's unintended credit that the nation is today indebted for the provision of the Copyright Law which states that "No copyright shall subsist in any publication of the United States Government." It was as a direct result of his improprieties that this prohibition was incorporated in Section 7 of the 1909 Copyright Act (35 Stat, 1077).

[6] Congress was undoubtedly unmindful of the Richardson incident and the Senate report when permission was given for copyrighting of the exhibits on pages 83 and 85. The recommendations of the Senate report are as pertinent today as they were in 1900.

[5] To this day, scholars and others who consult "The Messages and Papers of the Presidents" remain inhibited about quoting from this work. Despite the invalidation of Rep. Richardson's copyright, no practical way has yet been devised for removing copyright notices from works adjudged non-copyrightable after they have been placed in circulation.

10

WHAT'S OFFICIAL?

"No copyright shall subsist in the original text of any work which is in the public domain . . . or in any publication of the United States Government, or in any reprint in whole or in part thereof . . ."

If this portion of the Copyright Act is lacking in exactness, its essential purpose is nevertheless clear: the contents of governmental publications should not be subject to private copyright restrictions.

The Copyright Act obviously does not mean that government agencies may with impunity be party to the copyrighting of any work commissioned by these agencies or their officers.

The Copyright Act obviously does not mean that material prepared by a public servant at public expense can be transformed into his exclusive private property.

The Copyright Act obviously does not mean that material written expressly for the United States Government, printed (or processed) with machinery of that government, and publicized under the official imprimatur of that government can be placed under copyright restrictions.[1]

To all indications these considerations do not seem to deter or discourage extensive copyrighting by and through public officials—largely, but not exclusively, because exactly what is meant by the phrase "publication of the United States Government" is not defined in the Copyright Act. "This generalization," as the U. S. Court of Appeals pointed out in the Rickover case, "creates a sea of troublesome questions." [2] Unfortunately, the sea has in certain respects been greatly widened by the Court's rulings.

"The language of the original statute on printing—'No . . . Government publication shall be copyrighted'—seems to refer to a publication actually

---

[1] See footnote on page 13 for the author's statement regarding material of an official nature.

Admittedly not everything published by the government is official in every possible sense of the word. A privately prepared and duly copyrighted magazine article, for example, isn't divested of protection because it is quoted in a government publication.

The second half of Section 8 of the Copyright Act protects private copyrights against governmental use of copyrighted material: "The publication or republication by the government, either separately or in a public document, of any material in which copyright is subsisting shall not be taken to cause any abridgment or annulment of the copyright or to authorize any use or appropriation of such copyright material without the consent of the copyright proprietor."

[2] Page 8 of the Court's decision, October 20, 1960.

produced by the Public Printer. The Printing Office provision seems to mean, if read naturally, 'produced in that office.' The Copyright provision should be read, we think, to refer to publications commissioned or printed at the cost and direction of the United States. These would be authorized expositions on matters of governmental interest by governmental authority." [3]

While publication by the Government Printing Office is "a conveniently simple criterion upon which to base the definition of a government publication," as a member of the faculty of the George Washington University Law School has stated,[4] it is not a satisfactory criterion because innumerable pronouncements of government (and government officials) are today processed by myriad means. Distinctly conscious of this, the Superintendent of Documents has in recent years classified as official publications all processed material ("publications which are reproduced by duplicating processes . . . such as mimeograph, multigraph, planograph, rotaprint, multilith, etc.") emanating from government agencies, as well as all publications printed by the Government Printing Office.[5]

Accordingly, in the opinion of Herbert A. Howell, chief attorney of the Copyright Office for many years, any document, report, register, bulletin or circular issued by any governmental agency must be considered a government publication.[6]

An early definition, used by the Superintendent of Documents for many years as the basis for listing official publications, identified a government publication as *"Any publication printed at Government expense or published by authority of Congress or any Government Publishing Office . . ."* [7]

A definition provided by a Congressional committee in 1913 was as follows: "The term 'Government publication' . . . shall be held to mean and include all publications printed at Government expense or published or distributed by authority of Congress. No Government publication nor any portion thereof shall be copyrighted . . ." Pointing out that these words were consistent with the definition adopted by the Superintendent of Documents, a Senate Committee emphasized that use of the imprimatur of the issuing agency "makes it certain whether such matter is a Government publication." [8]

Based upon recommendations made by members of Congress, the Register of Copyrights, and others, the present phrasing of Section 8 of the

[3] Page 9 of the Court's decision in the Rickover case.

[4] "Piracy in High Places", Maurice B. Stiefel, George Washington Law Review, March, 1956.

[5] *Ibid.*

[6] The Copyright Law, Herbert A. Howell, 1952 edition, p. 45.

[7] Checklist of U.S. Public Documents, 1789-1909, 1911 edition, p. vii.

[8] Senate Report 438, p. 50; 63rd Congress, 2nd Session (1914).

THE DEPARTMENT OF STATE

Bulletin

THE
OFFICIAL
WEEKLY RECORD
OF
UNITED STATES
FOREIGN POLICY

Vol. XLIII, No. 1113   October 24, 1960

For index see inside back cover

Speeches by State Department officers are considered so official they are published regularly in the agency's "Official Weekly Record of United States Foreign Policy." Of the three items listed in the above typical issue two were addresses. Mr. Bohlen's speech was delivered at a program of Project Alert, a community education program sponsored by citizens of El Paso, Texas. Mr. Thayer's address was delivered before educators in Chicago. Under precedents established by Admiral Rickover, Messrs. Bohlen and Thayer could place copyright restrictions on such speeches despite their publication under the imprimatur of the official seal of the United States.

LIST OF SMITHSONIAN PUBLICATIONS AVAILABLE FOR DISTRIBUTION JUNE 30, 1958

COMPILED
BY
EILEEN M. McCARTHY

(Publication 4344)

CITY OF WASHINGTON
PUBLISHED BY THE SMITHSONIAN INSTITUTION
1958

Of the hundreds of publications published by the Smithsonian Institution few have been copyrighted although most of the authors are private individuals rather than public officials. Established with private funds and governed by a board including private citizens, Smithsonian could easily justify copyrighting. However, it adheres closely to the policy that works it publishes should not be subject to copyright restrictions. Scholars anxious to obtain the benefit of governmental auspices generally do not expect copyrighting privileges.

Copyright Act was the outgrowth of discussions that followed in the wake of the scandal evoked by the discovery that Rep. James D. Richardson had placed copyright restrictions on Presidential speeches printed with plates obtained from the Government Printing Office.[9]

Not long after the prohibitions of Section 8 went into effect, an eminent attorney stated:

"Thus, by express provision of statute, there can be no copyright in any publications of the United States Government and this would include its departments and officers, acting as officers. This would appear to be strictly in consonance with a sound public policy and declaratory of prior law. Thus, prior to the passage of the present Act, it had been held that copyright could not be obtained even by the judges.[10] In the opinion of judges or courts, Federal or State, or in statutes, although copyright might be obtained in leadnotes, not written by the judges, indices, abstracts of argument of counsel, annotations and pagination and arrangement by the reporter, of the matter set forth in such works.[11] While the states are not mentioned in this section, it may be questioned for the reasons underlying the decisions cited, whether any copyright may be obtained by any State, or State Officer, in any State paper or publication,[12] since a republic can only rest upon a firm basis if its citizens are afforded as untrammelled a means as possible of knowing its affairs and doings and communicating that knowledge to others, and since works composed by public officers in their official capacity, belong to the people whom they represent and who pay them for their services in making such compositions."[13]

In the light of the present inadequate phrasing of the Copyright Act the U.S. Court of Appeals took an important step in the right direction when it declared: "The Copyright provision should be read, we think, to refer to publications commissioned or printed at the cost and direction of the United States. These would be authorized expositions on matters of governmental interest by governmental authority."

But, unfortunately, the Court widened in certain respects the "sea of troublesome questions" arising out of the Copyright Act.

When is an act by a government officer "commissioned" by "the United States"? Are not acts performed or statements made by top echelon public officials usually commissioned or authorized by themselves in the course of carrying out their responsibilities? Would not the processes of government be greatly handicapped if key officials were stymied by the absence

---

[9] See pages 98-102 for details about the Richardson copyrights.
[10] Banks v. Manchester, 128 U.S. 245, 326 ed. 426.
[11] Callaghan v. Myers, 128 U.S. 617 32 L.ed. 547.
[12] Little v. Gould, 2 Blatch, 362.
[13] American Copyright Law, Arthur W. Weil, 1917, p. 246.

of specific authorization by "the United States" for each and every statement made and act performed? What are "matters of government interest by governmental authority"? Are governmental matters of interest to the public to be disregarded?

These are questions that must be taken into consideration in the revision of the Copyright Act.

The law of privilege as a defense by officers of government in civil suits relating to their official acts is one of long tradition. The Constitution specifically extends this privilege to members of Congress in respect to any speech, debate, report or action committed while the legislative bodies are in session.

The law of privilege for officials has for the most part been developed by the judiciary. The Supreme Court early held that government officers were privileged as respects actions or statements made by them in the course of carrying out their duties.[1]

In several recent cases—Barr v. Mateo [2] and Howard V. Lyons and McAteer[3]—the Supreme Court of the land has held that governmental press releases are government publications that enjoy the status of privileged documents and that the authorization of such releases is within the scope of a high official's discretionary duties even though he has not been specifically "commissioned" to undertake such authorization.

"The issuance of such releases," declared the Court with reference to the circumstances leading up to the Barr v. Mateo suit, "was standard agency practice, as it has become with many governmental agencies in these times. We think that under these circumstances a publicly expressed statement . . . was an appropriate exercise of the discretion which an officer of that rank must possess . . . It would be an unduly restrictive view of the scope of the duties of a policy-making executive official to hold that a public statement of agency policy in respect to matters of wide public interest and concern is not action in the line of duty. That petitioner was not *required* by law or by direction of his superiors to speak out cannot be controlling in the case of an official of policy-making rank, for the same considerations which underly the recognition of the privilege [of official statements in libel proceedings] as to acts done in connection with a mandatory duty apply with equal force to discretionary acts at those levels of government where the concept of duty encompasses the sound exercise of discretionary authority."

In the recent case of Ogden v. Association of the U.S. Army,[4] the doctrine of governmental privilege underwent unusually severe strain because of the contradictions that are inevitable when official material is trans-

[1] Bradley v. Fisher, 12 Wall, 335.
[2] 360 U.S. 564 (1959).
[3] 360 U.S. 593 (1959).

108

formed into private property by or through government officers. In this case Captain Lawrence J. Ogden sued Combat Forces Press for publishing allegedly libelous statements about him in "Combat Action in Korea". Evidence of the validity of his allegations was so strong that the defense strategy employed by the publisher's counsel centered on the contention that the book in question was published by Combat Forces Press by special arrangement with the Department of the Army, that it was an official publication of the United States, and that its contents were privileged despite the fact that it had been privately published.

[4] Civil Action 1735-59, U.S. District Court for the District of Columbia.

11

RICKOVER VERSUS THE PUBLIC

Compared to the copyrighting activities of other public officials those of
Admiral H. G. Rickover[1] are exceptional—and, in a sense, noteworthy—
chiefly because the circumstances surrounding and arising out of them dem-
onstrate quite clearly what can happen if copyrighting of a predominantly
official nature is not appropriately checked. From the public's viewpoint
they constitute an excellent test case through which to appraise the problem
of copyrighting by government officers.

The story begins on October 29, 1958. Public Affairs Press, a publishing organization specializing in the publication of pamphlets and books on
national affairs, requested of Admiral Rickover copies of several of his
public speeches prepared, processed, and distributed under the official
auspices of the Department of Defense[2] and the Atomic Energy Commission, in order to *quote* from these speeches.

[1] For chronological details regarding the Rickover copyrights see Washington Post
1-10-59, 1-27-59; Washington Evening Star 2-11-59; New York Times 10-24-59; Washington Evening Star 118-59, 10-20-60.

For briefs and court decisions see:

Brief For Public Affairs Press, Case 15,463, filed by Counsel Stanley B. Frosh with
the U.S. Court of Appeals for the District of Columbia, on February 10, 1960, 64 pp.

Reply Brief For Public Affairs Press, Case 15,463, filed by Counsel Stanley B. Frosh
with the U.S. Court of Appeals For the District of Columbia, on March 24, 1960,
14 pp.

Brief for Amicus Curiae, Sigma Delta Chi, Case 15,463, filed by Counsel Harry N.
Rosenfield with the U.S. Court of Appeals For the District of Columbia Circuit, on
March 29, 1960, 30 pp.

Brief for Admiral H. G. Rickover, Case 15,463, filed by Counsel Joseph A. McDonald,
Edwin S. Nail, Harry Buchman, Smith, Hennessey & McDonald with the U.S. Court
of Appeals For the District of Columbia, on March 10, 1960, 26 pp.

Decision of the U.S. District Court For the District of Columbia, Civil Action No.
116-59, October 23, 1959, 13 pp.

Decision of the U.S. Court of Appeals For the District of Columbia Circuit, Case
15,463, October 20, 1960, 21 pp.

For legal comments see Harvard Law Review, Recent Cases, Vol. 73, 1960, pp. 1219-
1222; University of Virginia Law Review, Recent Decisions, Vol. 46, 1960, pp. 137-
140; Columbia Law Review, Notes Section, Vol. 60, 1960, pp. 398-400; "Private Public
Utterances?", article by William H. Edwards, member of the Rhode Island Bar, Providence Journal, December 30, 1959.

For detailed editorial and other comment see Hartford Courant 5-18-59; Washington
Post 5-19-59, 10-28-59; 11-7-59, 10-21-60; Des Moines Register 11-3-59; Buffalo News
11-4-59; Dallas News 11-27-59; Providence, R.I., Journal 12-30-59; Muncie (Ind.)
Star 1-12-59; New York Daily News 2-12-59. See also pages 133-139 of this report.

UNITED STATES DISTRICT COURT

FOR THE DISTRICT OF COLUMBIA

PUBLIC AFFAIRS ASSOCIATES, INC.,

PLAINTIFF,

v.

CIVIL ACTION
NO. 116-59

VICE ADMIRAL HYMAN G. RICKOVER,

DEFENDANT.

OPINION

Stanley B. Frosh, of Washington, D. C., for the plaintiff.

Joseph A. McDonald, of Washington, D. C., for the defendant.

This is the trial of an action for a declaratory judgment. The case has been submitted on an agreed statement of facts supplemented by a number of documents that were introduced in evidence. The suit is brought by a publishing house against a Vice Admiral of the United States Navy, to secure an adjudication that would declare in effect that the defendant has no property right in his speeches; that they are not subject to copyright; that any one is free to publish them at will without paying him

Compare above with exhibits on pages 115 and 116. Which looks more official? Although the above is the first page of a federal court decision it appears to be far less official than the Defense Department and Atomic Energy Commission press releases that Admiral Rickover consider unofficial. Even announcements of executive orders of the President of the U. S. look less official.

125

Upon receipt of this request, Admiral Rickover adjured the Press that it could not *quote from these speeches in any way*.[3] It is of considerable importance that Admiral Rickover's position in this connection was unqualified, leaving no doubt whatsoever that his refusal applied to even the most meager of quotations.

Moreover, it is of considerable importance that four months previously, as subsequently became known, the Admiral had sold to E. P. Dutton and Company exclusive rights to the "Addresses of Admiral Rickover". This transaction took place on July 9, 1958.

Astonished that a highly placed and widely respected official could arbitrarily refuse to permit quotation from public speeches that had been officially prepared, processed and publicized, the editor of the Press decided to challenge the right of the Admiral to place any restrictions on these speeches or to sell to a private business company exclusive rights to their contents. Here, it seemed quite apparent, was a distinctly flagrant example of what was inevitable if government officers were to continue to use government resources for private purposes without regard to the guarantees of the Bill of Rights and the prohibitions of the Copyright Act.

In the controversy that ensued, the Press took the position that it had the right to publish the speeches in whole or in part. It took this position for the simple reason that it could not concede that although the speeches had been published as official publications of the Defense Department and the Atomic Energy Commission, Admiral Rickover could prohibit the Press from publishing texts of the speeches but did not have the right to forbid quotation of extracts from them. Moreover, it took the position that the Admiral could not grant to E. P. Dutton, the New York firm to which he had sold his speeches, exclusive rights to any matter originally prepared, published and disseminated as government publications.

On November 4, 1958, the Press advised the Admiral that since his speeches had been made in his official capacity, it saw no reason why it could not quote any of them in whole or in part. On this date the editor of the Press advised Admiral Rickover:

"In view of the fact that your speeches have been made in your official capacity, I can't believe that it is proper to restrict their use in any way. That sort of thing is, in my opinion, contrary to what the American people have come to expect of you.

"Quite frankly, we would be inclined to respect your wishes if you asked us not to use your speeches as a matter of courtesy, but in view of the position you have taken I see no proper reason why we should not have

[2] See Defense Department directive and Navy Department regulation on pages 39 through 43.

[3] Letter of October 31, 1958, letterhead of the Atomic Energy Commission.

as much opportunity to publish them in book from as any other private publishing house."

A week later, on November 10, 1958, the Admiral adjured the Press, in a telephone conversation with its Executive Director, not to quote any portion of his speeches and warned him that legal action would be taken against the Press if it did quote said speeches.

On November 12, 1958, the Press received from an authorized agent of Admiral Rickover a letter stating that any use of the speeches in question on the part of the Press would result in legal action on behalf of the Admiral.

On December 1, 1958, Admiral Rickover placed under his private copyright, via registration with the Copyright Office of the Library of Congress, 22 speeches that had been publicly delivered and officially disseminated in the previous four years. These speeches were covered by Copyright Registration A 363452.[4]

The text of all of the 22 speeches submitted to the Copyright Office had originally been distributed, without restriction, to members of the press and the public long prior to the date of attempted copyright. Virtually all of these speeches had been published as press release publications of the Defense Department and the Atomic Energy Commission. Moreover, when originally disseminated to the press and other persons who might care to quote from or print them, most of the speeches bore the official imprimaturs of the Department of Defense and the Atomic Energy Commission. In addition to distribution by the press offices of the Department of Defense and the Atomic Energy Commission, copies of these speeches were distributed by Admiral Rickover through official facilities of the U.S. Government available to him. There is no evidence or indication whatsoever that the Admiral did not desire maximum publicity for these speeches. There was at no time any restriction on their publication, in whole or in part, by anyone.

When, however, the speeches were submitted to the Copyright Office on December 1, 1958, their original press release form was not shown and the official imprimaturs of the Defense Department and the Atomic Energy Commission were missing. In all other respects, the speeches were identical with those originally published and publicized at the instance of Admiral Rickover by agencies of the United States Government.

Although the four speeches made by Admiral Rickover *after* December 1, 1958, were submitted to the Copyright Office for registration prior to their delivery, there is no evidence that they were not prepared during official hours with official intelligence and resources. Nor is there any evidence that they were private, not official, expressions of Admiral Rick-

[4] See exhibit on page 121.

Rickover Puts Copyright Stamp on Slated Speech

United Press International

Vice Adm. Hyman G. Rickover, never one to yield blindly to tradition, raised some eyebrows yesterday by fixing a copyright stamp on a speech he will deliver in New York Thursday.

Asked whether Government officials or others on the public payroll could copyright their speeches, Rickover said he had not consulted a lawyer about it, but felt strongly that he certainly had the legal

In addition, Rickover said he provided money to have the speech mimeographed and did not use Government facilities.

mission. He also said he paid for having the speech prepared for distribution.

Rickover distributed copies of his speech with this notation on Page 1:

"Copyright 1958, H. G. Rickover.

"No permission needed for contemporaneous press use. Above copyright notice to be used if most of speech reprinted."

Question Raised

The question whether Rickover had a right to forbid publication of a collection of his official Navy speeches was raised last month by M. B. Schnapper, executive director of the Public Affairs Press.

Schnapper, who said Rickover had denied his firm permission to publish such speeches, accused the Admiral of challenging "the privilege of a free press to use unclassi-

his official duties, which deal with nuclear propulsion. In addition, Rickover said he provided money to have the speech mimeographed and did not use Government facilities.

Rickover did not indicate whether he would follow the same procedure with future speeches he may make on subjects connected with his Government work. He indicated he felt he also could copyright such speeches.

A lawyer at the Defense Department gave this off-the-cuff opinion on the matter:

If a military official gives a speech on a military matter in his official capacity, then it becomes public property. Anyone can publish it without fear of infringing on a copyright.

If, however, the official makes a speech on a subject

Extracts from a Washington Post story of December 10, 1958. According to Reporter Tom Nelson the Admiral said he "provided money to have the speech mimeographed and did not use Government facilities". This was refuted on January 22, 1959, in the letter reproduced on the next page. Moreover, it was contradicted by the Admiral himself in the Statement of Facts his attorney submitted to the U. S. District Court on October 14, 1959.

22 January 1959

The President
Public Affairs Press
419 New Jersey Avenue, S.E.

Dear Sir;

    As a matter of information you may be interested to know that
in connection with the Rickover matter there was some misinformation
concerning who,where, when, and on what machines this speech was
produced. The speech was written during Government time, on government paper, on a government typewriter, and reproduced on government mimeograph machines. All Clerks including one Warrant Officer
employed in that office have served notice that they would tell the
truth about the entire matter if required to do so in court. We feel
as you do concerning publication of a speech of this type.

An anonymous letter received by Public Affairs Press shortly after publication of the Washington Post story relating that Admiral Rickover had stated that the copyrighted speeches in question had been processed at his own expense and did not involve the use of governmental facilities. The writer of the letter appeared to have an intimate knowledge of distinctly pertinent facts. According to a United Press dispatch of January 27, 1959, the Navy Department promised to investigate the assertions made in the letter but no findings were made public. Efforts to establish the exact facts were prevented when Judge Holtzoff ruled that he was averse to questioning of Admiral Rickover by the attorney of Public Affairs Press. In a statement submitted to the U. S. District Court by Admiral Rickover's attorney on October 14, 1959, it was conceded that "All of the speeches were multilithed on Government duplicating machines." Note exhibits on pages 119, 120.

The basic position of Public Affairs Press is that it was altogether proper for the Admiral to use official facilities and resources since his speeches were necessarily official statements. Why, however, the Admiral informed United Press that he had personally provided money to have the material processed and did not use Government facilities remains unexplained. Accuracy of the UP story was never challenged.

NEWS RELEASE
PLEASE NOTE DATE

DEPARTMENT OF DEFENSE
OFFICE OF PUBLIC INFORMATION
Washington 25, D. C.

FOR RELEASE AT 11:00 A.M. (PST)
THURSDAY, OCTOBER 27, 1955

Remarks Prepared by RADM H. G. Rickover, USN
Chief, Naval Reactors Branch
Division of Reactor Development
U. S. Atomic Energy Commission
and
Assistant Chief of the Bureau of Ships
for Nuclear Propulsion
Navy Department
For Delivery at Luncheon Sponsored by
The San Francisco Council of the Navy League,
The Chamber of Commerce, and
The Commercial Club
Merchants Exchange Building
San Francisco, California
October 27, 1955

NUCLEAR POWER AND THE NAVY

I appreciate this opportunity to talk to you on Theodore Roosevelt's birthday because he, more than any other man, helped to mold our Navy into a highly mechanized and effective instrument of national policy. In particular, he encouraged the Navy to convert from coal to oil. Although the use of oil as a fuel for our warships had been under consideration since 1866, it was not until his administration, and with his encouragement and support, that the final decision to change was made — a change almost as significant as the one from sail to coal.

Today our Navy is embarked on an even grater change — from oil to nuclear power. I don't believe this will take as long as it took to convert from sail to steam or from coal to oil. Unlike the earlier changes in which merchant shipping took the lead, the change to nuclear power began with a naval vessel.

Title page of one of the Rickover speeches covered by Copyright Registration A363452. Note official seal of the Defense Department. The U. S. Court of Appeals ruled on Oct. 20, 1960, that despite the government imprimatur, the seal of the Department of Defense, and the official press release nature of this and a score of other speeches by the Admiral they could have been placed under Rickover's personal copyright if he had complied with copyright procedures.

UNITED STATES
ATOMIC ENERGY COMMISSION
Washington 25, D. C.

Tel. ST 3-8000   FOR RELEASE AT 9:00 P.M. (EDT)
Ext. 307   TUESDAY, MAY 14, 1957

Remarks Prepared by RADM H. G. Rickover, USN
Chief, Naval Reactors Branch
Division of Reactor Development
U. S. Atomic Energy Commission
and
Assistant Chief of the Bureau of Ships
for Nuclear Propulsion
Navy Department
For Delivery at Banquet of the
Annual Scientific Assembly of the
Minnesota State Medical Association
St. Paul, Minnesota
May 14, 1957

—————————————

ENERGY RESOURCES AND OUR FUTURE

I am honored to be here tonight, though it is
no easy thing, I assure you, for a layman to face up to
an audience of physicians. A single one of you, sitting
behind his desk, can be quite formidable.

My speech has no medical connotations. This may
be a relief to you after the solid professional fare you
have been absorbing. I should like to discuss a matter
which will, I hope, be of interest to you as responsible
citizens: the significance of energy resources in the
shaping of our future.

One of the 22 speeches Admiral Rickover placed under
Copyright Registration A 363452. Note the imprimatur
of the U. S. Atomic Energy Commission and the telephone
number of the information officer of that agency.

over. Accompanying three of the speeches was the following notice: "Copyright [1958 and 1959], H. G. Rickover. No permission needed for contemporaneous press use. Above copyright notice to be used if most of speech reprinted."

When the Admiral's copyrights on these speeches were protested by V. M. Newton, Jr., Chairman of the National Freedom of Information Committee of Sigma Delta Chi, the professional journalistic fraternity, Admiral Rickover advised Mr. Newton: "To place any limitation on the publication of thinking, whether it be my thinking or that of anyone else, is the exact opposite of my desire." Subsequently the Admiral inserted the following phrasing in the copyright notice appended to his speech entitled "The Shippingport Atomic Power Station: Lessons From Its Operation": "No permission needed for newspaper or news periodical use."

All of the speeches Admiral Rickover submitted to the Copyright Office were prepared on government time, with the use of government personnel and government facilities, and contained official information obtained by him in his official capacity. A list of the speeches, the dates on which they were delivered, and the names of the agencies of the United States Government that publicized and disseminated them as press releases appears on pages 119 and 120.

All of Admiral Rickover's applications for registration of copyright on the speeches listed, as the name and the address of the party who manufactured them as publications, Theresa Leone, an employee of the federal government, assigned to the Admiral for assistance in the conduct of his official duties. At all material times, the Admiral was a full time official of the Department of Defense assigned variously to duties with the Navy Department and the Atomic Energy Commission. There is no indication in any of his speeches that he was speaking in other than his official capacity.

In view of a number of surprising representations made by Admiral Rickover in the course of a telephone conversation with him on November 10, 1958, the editor of the Press posed the following question in a letter he sent the Admiral on the following day:

"Are your speeches being made in your official or private capacity? In what capacity are they prepared by you? Are they mimeographed officially or privately? If they can be freely published in newspapers why can't they be published in books without any restrictions?"

These questions remained unanswered as of January 16, 1959, when the Press requested the United States District Court for a declaratory judgment on the issues presented.

CONSTRAINT BY COPYRIGHT

As published by the Defense Department and the Atomic Energy Commission, the press releases containing the speeches by Admiral Rickover are official publications of the United States Government, it was contended by Public Affairs Press in presentation of its case by attorney Stanley B. Frosh before the U.S. Court of Appeals for the District of Columbia Circuit.

If these press releases are official publications then, regardless of all other considerations, they cannot possibly be subject to copyright restrictions. The Copyright Act unequivocally states: "No copyright shall subsist in the original text of . . . any publication of the United States Government."

As is amply evident in the exhibits of the case, the press releases at issue are unquestionably publications of the United States Government. They are official in every essential respect—in content, in subject matter, in information, in preparation, in processing, in dissemination, in authorship, and in imprimatur. The only respect in which they are "unofficial" is in the assertion to this effect made belatedly by Admiral Rickover in what was presumably his "unofficial" capacity.

Singly and collectively, all the characteristics of the press releases are the standard characteristics of government publications. Although the texts of enactments by Congress and Executive Orders by the President might be considered *more* official, this would not be readily evident in a comparison of such documents with the publications at issue. It can indeed be said (and seen) that many official publications—including copies of the various court decisions in the case—are far less official in appearance and phrasing than the press releases of Admiral Rickover's speeches.

If publications that appear to be and are official can be sanctioned as private, then, it was emphasized by Mr. Frosh, private publications appearing under official guise could be considered justifiable by persons seeking to misrepresent private matter as official.

As exhibits and other evidence in the record show, all but several of the speeches by Admiral Rickover were originally published as press release publications of the Defense Department and the Atomic Energy Commission with the full benefit of (1) official auspices, (2) official resources, and (3) official facilities in every practical and essential respect.

Official auspices are most conspicuously evident in the official imprimaturs of the Defense Department and the Atomic Energy Commission appearing on most of the press releases. No one seeing these imprimaturs could possibly doubt their significance and the official nature of the material they included.

Metallurgy In Atomic Power	October 20, 1955
(Atomic Energy Commission)	
Nuclear Power and the Navy	October 27, 1955
(Defense Department)	
Engineering and Scientific Education	November 22, 1955
(Atomic Energy Commission)	
Lead Time and Military Strength	January 12, 1956
(Defense Department)	
Nuclear Power and the Navy	August 16, 1956
(Defense Department)	
The Education of Our Talented Children	November 20, 1956
(Atomic Energy Commission)	
Nuclear Power—Challenge to Industry	January, 1957
(Defense Department)	
The Challenge of Nuclear Power	March 1, 1957
(Defense Department)	
The Talented Mind	March 11, 1957
(Defense Department)	
Energy Resources and Our Future	May 14, 1957
(Atomic Energy Commission)	
The Naval Revolution	September 14, 1957
(Defense Department)	
Acceptance of International Communication Award	
(Defense Department, announcement)	October 12, 1957
The Balance Sheet on Education	November 22, 1957
(Atomic Energy Commission)	
Revolution at Sea	December 5, 1957
(Defense Department)	
Education in the Nuclear Age	December 6, 1957
(Atomic Energy Commission)	
European and American Secondary Schools	March 23, 1958
(Atomic Energy Commission)	
The Truth Shall Make You Free	April 19, 1958
(Atomic Energy Commission)	
The Meaning of Your Profession	June 14, 1958
(Atomic Energy Commission)	
Investment in Human Resources	September 25, 1958
(Atomic Energy Commission)	
The Meaning of the Nautilus' Polar Voyage	September 29, 1958
(Atomic Energy Commission)	

A list of speeches Admiral H. G. Rickover placed under copyright despite the fact that they had been issued as press releases of the Atomic Energy Commission and the Defense Department. Official imprimaturs of these agencies and the various titles of Admiral Rickover as an official of both the Atomic Energy Commission and the Navy Department appeared on all of the above.

(Continued on next page)

Continuation of the list of press releases copyrighted by Admiral Rickover. The last few items were presumably processed privately. For details regarding the "Shippingport Atomic Power Station; Lessons From Its Operation" see page 127.

Nuclear Power Only Answer

A Crisis in the Fossil Fuel Era

By VICE ADMIRAL HYMAN G. RICKOVER

We live in what historians may some day call the Fossil Fuel Age. Today coal, oil, and natural gas supply 93 per cent of the world's energy; water power accounts for only 1 per cent; and the labor of men and domestic animals the remaining 6 per cent. This is a startling reversal of corresponding figures for 1850. Then fossil fuels supplied 5 per cent of the world's energy, and men and animals 94 per cent. Five-sixths of all the coal, oil, and gas consumed since the beginning of the Fossil Fuel Age has been burned up in the last 55 years.

These fuels have been known to man for more than 3000 years. In parts of China, coal was used for domestic heating and cooking, and natural gas for lighting as early as 1000 B. C. The Babylonians burned asphalt a thousand years earlier. But these early uses were sporadic and of

What's ahead in fuels is vital to the civilized world. Here, one of the leading authorities on the subject gives his views. What he says is alarming but the situation isn't hopeless. Vice Admiral Hyman G. Rickover, father of the first American A-powered submarine, gave The Washington Daily News permission to reprint, in part, a recent and timely speech on the world fuel crisis, of interest to everybody, the scientist and layman alike, everywhere in the free world.

The next important high-energy converter used by Europeans was gun powder—an energy source far superior to the muscular strength of the strongest bowman or lancer.

Extract from the Washington Daily News of March 1, 1960. Note that box at right explains that Admiral Rickover's speech on nuclear fuels is printed with the Admiral's permission. Such observance of the Admiral's copyrights constitutes recognition that a government officer has a legal right to prevent newspapers from quoting what he has said in his official capacity. Nuclear fuels are a major concern of the Admiral as Chief of the Naval Reactors Branch of the Atomic Energy Commission and as the Navy's Assistant Chief of the Bureau of Ships for Nuclear Propulsion.

7. If registration fee is to be charged to a deposit account established in the Copyright Office, give name of account:

8. Name and address of person or organization to whom correspondence or refund, if any, should be sent:

Name .... Address ....

9. Send certificate to:

(Type or print
name and address)

Name	HYMAN GEORGE RICKOVER
Address	4801 Connecticut Avenue, N.W.
	(Number and street)
	Washington, D.C.
	(City) (Zone) (State)

10. **Certification:** (NOTE: Application not acceptable unless signed)

I CERTIFY that the statements made by me in this application are correct to the best of my knowledge.

H. G. Rickover

(Signature of copyright claimant or duly authorized agent)

11. **Affidavit (required by law).** Instructions: (1) Fill in the blank spaces with special attention to those marked "(X)." (2) Sign the affidavit before an officer authorized to administer oaths within the United States, such as a notary public. (3) Have the officer sign and seal the affidavit and fill in the date of execution.

NOTE: The affidavit must be signed and notarized only *on or after* the date of publication or completion of printing which it states. The affidavit must be signed by an individual.

STATE OF ....
District of Columbia } ss:
COUNTY OF ....

I, the undersigned, depose and say that I am the

☒ Person claiming copyright in the book described in this application;

☐ The duly authorized agent of the person or organization claiming copyright in the book described in this application;

☐ The printer of the book described in this application.

That the book was published or the printing was completed on: (X) ....November 28, 1958....

(Give, month, day, and year)

That of the various processes employed in the production of the copies deposited, the setting of the type and the making of plates, or the lithographic or photoengraving processes used in producing the text, were performed within the limits of the United States, and that the printing of the text and the binding (if any) were also performed within the limits of the United States. That these processes were performed by the following establishments or individuals at the following addresses:
(GIVE THE NAMES AND ADDRESSES OF THE PERSONS OR ORGANIZATIONS WHO PRODUCED THE COPIES—TYPESETTERS, PRINTERS, BINDERS, ETC.)

Names (X) ..Theresa Leone........   Addresses (X) ..924 25th Street, N.W., Washington, D.C.

H. G. Rickover

(Signature of affiant)

(Sign and notarize only on or *after* date given above)

PLACE
NOTARIAL SEAL
HERE

Subscribed and sworn to / affirmed before me this ....first....

day of ..December.............. 19 58

Katharine A. Thomason

(Signature of notary)

Signature page of Copyright Registration A 363451 filed by Admiral Rickover on December 1, 1958. Technically this covered the first of the speeches the Admiral placed under copyright restrictions. However, five months previously (on July 9, 1958) he asserted common law copyright ownership of the speeches when he sold to E. P. Dutton and Company exclusive publishing rights to the "Addresses of Admiral Rickover". Note that in this registration the Admiral swore that the "various processes employed in the production of the copies deposited" had been performed by Miss Theresa Leone of 924 - 25th Street, N.W., Washington, D. C. This does not jibe with the information in the letter received by Public Affairs Press on January 23, 1959, or with the Statement of Facts his attorney submitted to the U. S. District Court on October 14, 1959.

7. If registration fee is to be charged to a deposit account established in the Copyright Office, give name of account:

8. Name and address of person or organization to whom correspondence or refund, if any, should be sent:

Name .... Address ....

9. Send certificate to:

(Type or print
name and address)

Name .... HYMAN GEORGE RICKOVER ....

Address .... 4801 Connecticut Avenue, N.W. ....
(Number and street)

.... Washington, D.C. ....
(City)   (Zone)   (State)

10. **Certification:** (NOTE: Application not acceptable unless signed)
I CERTIFY that the statements made by me in this application are correct to the best of my knowledge.

H. G. Rickover
(Signature of copyright claimant or duly authorized agent)

11. **Affidavit (required by law).** Instructions: (1) Fill in the blank spaces with special attention to those marked "(X)."
(2) Sign the affidavit before an officer authorized to administer oaths within the United States, such as a notary public. (3) Have the officer sign and seal the affidavit and fill in the date of execution.

NOTE: The affidavit must be signed and notarized only *on or after* the date of publication or completion of printing which it states. The affidavit must be signed by an individual.

STATE OF ....
District of Columbia } ss:
COUNTY OF ....

I, the undersigned, depose and say that I am the
☒ Person claiming copyright in the book described in this application;

☐ The duly authorized agent of the person or organization claiming copyright in the book described in this application;

☐ The printer of the book described in this application.

That the book was published or the printing was completed on: (X) ....November 25, 1958.........
(Give, month, day, and year)

That of the various processes employed in the production of the copies deposited, the setting of the type and the making of plates, or the lithographic or photoengraving processes used in producing the text, were performed within the limits of the United States, and that the printing of the text and the binding (if any) were also performed within the limits of the United States. That these processes were performed by the following establishments or individuals at the following addresses:
(GIVE THE NAMES AND ADDRESSES OF THE PERSONS OR ORGANIZATIONS WHO PRODUCED THE COPIES—
TYPESETTERS, PRINTERS, BINDERS, ETC.)

Names (X) ....Theresa Leone........................ Addresses (X)924 25th Street, N.W., Washington, D.C.

H. G. Rickover
(Signature of affiant)
(Sign and notarize only on or after date given above)

PLACE
NOTARIAL SEAL
HERE

Subscribed and sworn to / affirmed before me this ....first........

day of ....December........................, 19 58.

Kathryn A. Thompson
(Signature of notary)

FOR COPYRIGHT OFFICE USE ONLY

The signature portion of the copyright Admiral Rickover placed on 22 speeches he delivered between 1954 and 1958. According to the Admiral's sworn assertions in this document, Theresa Leone of 924 - 25th Street, N.W., Washington, D. C., performed "the various processes employed in the production of the copies deposited", including "the setting of the type", "making of plates", and "binding". Miss Leone was apparently an employee of the Navy Department at about the time the above copyright was registered. In view of the large amount of material involved and the various production techniques involved it seems doubtful that Miss Leone performed all of the work credited to her, but it is not completely impossible. Was the work for which she is credited performed in her official capacity as an aide assigned to the Admiral or did she do it for the Admiral in her private capacity? Was the equipment she used located at 924 - 25th Street, N.W., Washington, D. C., or was it stationed in government offices?

Official auspices are plainly evident in heading matter such as the following:

DEPARTMENT OF DEFENSE
OFFICE OF PUBLIC INFORMATION
WASHINGTON 25, D. C.
UNITED STATES ATOMIC ENERGY COMMISSION
WASHINGTON 25, D. C.

Official auspices are made distinctly evident in conspicuous listing of the various official titles of Admiral Rickover. Note, for example, that in the case of the speech entitled "Nuclear Power and the Navy," the following lines appear underneath the Defense Department's imprimatur:

Remarks Prepared by RADM H. G. Rickover, USN
Chief, Naval Reactors Branch
Division of Reactor Development
U. S. Atomic Energy Commission
and
Assistant Chief of the Bureau of Ships
for Nuclear Propulsion
Navy Department

Official auspices were necessarily involved when press and information officers and personnel of the Defense Department, the Atomic Energy Commission, and the Navy Department made the press releases public and made copies of them available, without any restrictions whatsoever, to the press and to the public.

Official auspices were also involved when Admiral Rickover, acting in his official capacity, distributed or authorized distribution of copies of the press releases through official channels and under official frank.

Official resources used by Admiral Rickover are plainly evident in the subjects and contents of the speeches incorporated in the press releases. Without the official resources of the Defense Department, the Navy Department and the Atomic Energy Commission that are available to him—and to few others in the entire nation—the Admiral could not speak authoritatively on such matters as naval affairs, submarine warfare, nuclear propulsion, national defense, military policies, the armed forces, manpower problems, the menace of Soviet Russia, and the relationship of these matters to the nation's educational system.

Were it not for the official nature of his knowledge of these subjects, it is hardly likely that he would have been requested to deliver addresses on them at the United States Naval Submarine Base, the Navy's Guided Missile Preview Luncheon, a meeting of the Naval Affairs Committee of the American Legion, and a convention of the American Public Power

Association. At the last named occasion the subject of the Admiral's speech was "The Shippingport Atomic Power Station: Lessons From Its Operation." As is well known, at least partly as a result of his speeches, the Admiral is considered the father of the Shippingport Atomic Power Station as well as of the nuclear submarine.

Official resources are available to Admiral Rickover that are not and cannot be made available to private individuals. For this very reason alone, apart from others, he ought not use such resources for any private purpose whatsoever. As one of the highest officers of the Navy Department and the Atomic Energy Commission he is a privileged public servant who should not use his post to private advantage in any way prejudicial to the right of every citizen to be kept informed by a press that is not circumscribed by Government or by Government officials.

Official resources readily accessible to Admiral Rickover are not limited in scope or subject matter. As one of the nation's highest and most trusted officials he can draw upon the resources of virtually every agency of government at every level—national, state and local—on well nigh any subject relating to governmental responsibilities.

Official resources of the United States Government have been the primary basis of Admiral Rickover's extensive knowledge about national and international affairs ever since he entered the Government service 40 years ago. This is both implicitly and explicitly evident in his speeches. In the case of the Shippingport speech, for example, he quotes at length from a Government contract subject to his official approval.

Official facilities used by Admiral Rickover in processing and delivering his speeches may well be "a minor consideration," as his counsel has contended, but it is questionable, if not doubtful, that he would have used such facilities if he did not consider his efforts and requirements in this connection to be of an official nature. Moreover, if the nature of the facilities used is "a minor consideration," this applies not only to the speeches copyrighted prior to December 1, 1958, but also to the speeches copyrighted subsequently.

In refusing to permit Public Affairs Press to quote so much as a sentence from his speeches, Admiral Rickover not only abridged the Constitutional rights of the Press, but also violated the fundamental right of the American people to a free and unfettered press.

Since the nation's judiciary has traditionally acted unequivocally in disapproval of acts infringing upon freedom of press, it is altogether understandable that the Admiral's counsel should endeavor to persuade the court that such infringement is in no way involved, that such infringement has not occurred, and that such infringement was never intended. *As the record shows, however, the Admiral's acts were exactly to the contrary.*

PUBLIC AFFAIRS ASSOCIATES, INC.,

PLAINTIFF,

V.

VICE ADMIRAL HYMAN G. RICKOVER,

DEFENDANT.

CIVIL ACTION
NO. 116-59

OPINION

Stanley B. Frosh, of Washington, D. C., for the plaintiff.

Joseph A. McDonald, of Washington, D. C., for the defendant.

This is the trial of an action for a declaratory judgment. The case has been submitted on an agreed statement of facts supplemented by a number of documents that were introduced in evidence. The suit is brought by a publishing house against a Vice Admiral of the United States Navy, to secure an adjudication that would declare in effect that the defendant has no property right in his speeches; that they are not subject to copyright; that any one is free to publish them at will without paying him

Compare above with exhibits on pages 115 and 116. Which looks more official? Although the above is the first page of a federal court decision it appears to be far less official than the Defense Department and Atomic Energy Commission press releases that Admiral Rickover consider unofficial. Even announcements of executive orders of the President of the U. S. look less official.

CONSTRAINT BY COPYRIGHT

On October 29, 1958, Public Affairs Press informed Admiral Rickover that it planned to *"quote"* from speeches by him that had been published as official press release publications. Acting officially in behalf of the Admiral and with his authorization, his secretary advised the Press on October 31, 1958 that it could not be given permission to *"quote"* any portion of the Admiral's speeches. It is of considerable importance that the Admiral's position in this connection was unqualified, leaving no doubt whatsoever that his refusal applied to even the most meager of quotations.

Subsequently the Press took the position that it had the right to publish the speeches in whole or in part for the reasons set forth on page 111 and elsewhere in this report. If, declared the Press in its initial complaint to the court, Admiral Rickover could "restrict quotation from his public speeches, either in full or in part . . . once they have been delivered publicly" he could curtail both freedom of speech and press.

That the Admiral refused to permit the Press to publish extracts from the officially disseminated speeches he placed under his private copyright is a factor of the greatest importance.

Disregarding all the evidence demonstrating that the case had its roots in the refusal of Admiral Rickover to let the Press quote so much as a sentence from any of the 26 speeches he had placed under copyright registrations, the Admiral's attorney proceeded to interpret the Copyright Act as a statute so broad, so loose, and so permissive as to sanction all sorts of liberties detrimental to a copyright holder. Customarily this approach has been employed by parties charged with violating the Copyright Act.

Significantly, even if Admiral Rickover desired to permit quotation of any of his speeches by the Defense Department or the Atomic Energy Commission, he cannot grant such permission either as author or as copyright owner. Under the terms of his arrangement with Dutton he sold that firm exclusive publishing rights to the "Addresses of Admiral Rickover", retaining for himself copyright control only insofar as the movies and broadcasting are concerned. Moreover, it is significant that the lower court's decision did not sanction any type of quotation from Admiral Rickover's speeches without his express permission as copyright owner. Nor was quotation sanctioned by the United States Appeals Court validation of his copyrights on several speeches it considered his exclusive private property.

Contrary to the impression the Admiral's attorney has sought to create, it is not and has not been the contention of Public Affairs Press that the book "Education and Freedom" *as such* is at issue in the case.

FOR RELEASE AT 10:30 A.M. (PST)
THURSDAY, MAY 28, 1959

Remarks prepared by VADM H. G. Rickover, USN

for delivery at

The American Public Power Association Convention
Seattle, Washington
May 28, 1959

****

THE SHIPPINGPORT ATOMIC POWER STATION

LESSONS FROM ITS OPERATION

The purpose of the Shippingport project is stated in the
contract between the U. S. Atomic Energy Commission and the
Duquesne Light Company as follows:

"It is anticipated by the parties that the
information to be gained by the construction and
operation of the Pressurized Water Reactor will
probably permit a major advance toward realization
of civilian nuclear power and that such information
is expected to lead to further technical advances in
subsequent power reactors. It is recognized that this
first full-scale nuclear power plant will be of a
developmental nature and will be operated with the
primary objective of gaining information and advancing
reactor technology rather than with an objective of
furnishing dependable power and maintaining a high
load factor."

Although this speech relates directly to the duties of Admiral
Rickover as a top official of the Atomic Energy Commission
(he is credited with being the father of the Shippingport
Atomic Power Station), it has a valid copyright under the
ruling of the U. S. Court of Appeals. Note that the speech
appears to lean heavily on the contract between the U. S.
Atomic Energy Commission and the Duquesne Light Company. The nature of the contract was known to few at the
time the speech was delivered. The text of a different speech
before the American Public Power Association by another
AEC officer was an official non-copyrighted statement.

CONSTRAINT BY COPYRIGHT

As is pointed out in the Press' brief, "it is conceded that Admiral Rickover may have 'some' copyright protection in such new and original matter he may have privately added to the speeches for book publication purposes"—provided, of course, that such new and original matter was prepared without the benefit of governmental auspices, resources, and facilities.

What is at issue in regard to this book is the copyrightability of such of its contents as are merely or primarily reprints of press releases published by the Department of Defense and the Atomic Energy Commission. The Copyright Act expressly states with reference to reprints of Government publications: "No copyright shall subsist . . . in any publication of the United States Government, or any *reprint* in whole or in part, thereof."

On the first page of the first chapter of the book its contents are thus described: "This book is a collection of speeches made during the last four years." All of the speeches in the book were originally press release publications of the United States Department of Defense and the Atomic Energy Commission. Quotation of such material, in whole or in part, cannot and should not be prohibited.

Admiral Rickover's copyrights are detrimental to the interests of the United States Government and contrary to the policies and practices of the Defense Department. This is plainly evident in the documents reprinted or quoted on pages 39-43 as well as elsewhere in this report.

Like his copyrighted speeches on naval affairs and atomic energy, Admiral Rickover's addresses pertaining to education are closely related to his official concerns and responsibilities and those of the Navy Department and the Atomic Energy Commission. Throughout these speeches there is constant emphasis on his official duties, experience, observations, and knowledge. Moreover, the major themes of these speeches are national defense and democracy, the educational shortcomings of naval personnel, the requirements of technological warfare, and the superior military might of Soviet Russia because of educational factors.

Typical of the contents of these speeches is the following extract from "Education—Our First Line of National Defense":

"I have interviewed more than two thousand young men in the last twelve years, all top men in their college class. My naval reactor engineering group presently numbers about 150. Since the men who came to see me had already passed through a numbeer of previous interviews where all but the best were eliminated, it is evident that those who could not meet the requirements of the nuclear power project—and hence inferentially of any new development project—vastly outnumbered those who qualified . . .

Remarks prepared by VADM H. G. Rickover, USN
Assistant Director for Naval Reactors
Division of Reactor Development
U.S. Atomic Energy Commission
and
Assistant Chief of the Bureau of Ships
for Nuclear Propulsion
Navy Department
for delivery at
Special Convocation of
Indiana University
Bloomington, Indiana
March 20, 1960

RUSSIA VERSUS THE UNITED STATES--THE NATURE OF THE CONTEST

The gravest problem facing the government and people of the United States today is the contest forced upon us by the totalitarian bloc, captained by Soviet Russia. The need to hold our own in this contest aggravates all our national problems. No final solutions are in sight. We must keep on meeting the totalitarian challenge for as far into the future as we can presently foresee. Nothing we do to solve other problems will avail if we fail in this contest. Its outcome determines whether we survive as an independent democratic nation.

If we are to take intelligent and resolute action that will insure survival we must have a clear conception of what the contest is about. It is difficult, however, to muster the necessary detachment and breadth of view since this is a conflict between two diametrically opposed types of society and we are personally identified with one of them. The temptation is great to see it as nothing more complicated than Evil bent on destroying Good.

Title page of "Russia vs. the United States—the Nature of the Contest" a speech Admiral Rickover placed under his private copyright. While it's possible that the Admiral complied with statutory copyright procedures in this particular instance, it's an open question whether the highest interests of the United States are served when a top defense official places copyright restrictions on his knowledge of "the gravest problem facing the government and people of the United States". Note that although a disclaimer is made with regard to the Navy Department none is made concerning the U. S. Atomic Energy Commission. Was the phrasing intended to signify that the speech reflected the views of the Commission?

RICKOVER'S DISREGARD FOR DEMOCRACY

*Extracts from a speech by Mrs. Agnes E. Meyer before
the Association For Supervision and Curriculum
Development on March 6, 1960.*

"*Admiral Rickover's recommendation that we build 'brains
rather than character' in our schools is positively shocking
at a time when this country needs character in its citizens and
its leadership as never before. He does not realize how dangerous it would be to produce a group of experts lacking a
sense of social, moral, and cultural responsibility.*

"To be sure we need more scientists and engineers but we
also need vast numbers of highly competent leaders in every
area of human endeavor, especially in the field of public
administration. But *they must be leaders who understand
democratic ideals and methods; for neither the one nor the
other does Admiral Rickover show much sympathy.*

"*He shows his greatest disregard for democracy when he
suggests that we imitate the Russian system of education in
which the individual is treated as a tool of the state.* To be
sure the National Defense Education Act of 1958 is already
a step in that direction since it leads our children to think
that they are being educated not for their own unique development but primarily for national defense.

"In a democracy education must treat each child as an
authentic individual, not as a means to an end, not even so
important an end as the nation's security. I hope educators
will never be supine enough to accept military requirements
as paramount in determining the content of the curriculum.
If [they] do, we shall not only undermine our democratic
principles, but we shall not even reach the desired goal—the
maximum power of which our people are capable.

"Instead of following Admiral Rickover's advice to imitate
the authoritarian methods of Russia, we must develop an
education and a philosophy of education which will serve
the purposes of a free society as effectively as Soviet education
serves the purposes of despotism.

"Admiral Rickover . . . reveals a deep-seated hostility to
individual freedom at a moment when the struggle to maintain
freedom even here at home is more acute than ever. We
must bear in mind that our democratic principles are being
challenged not only by the communists. . . . "

Navy Seeks Teen-Agers for Nuclear Subs

By JIM G. LUCAS
Scripps-Howard Staff Writer

The Navy is recruiting teen-agers from the nation's high schools to man its nuclear submarines.

The personnel bureau has its sights on a 1960 quota of 2000 specially selected, high-IQ graduates for its regular nuclear submarine program, and another 650 for special training in Polaris IRBM and Polaris submarine operations. It is particularly interested in boys who have majored in math or physics.

1200 IN

Last year, it recruited 1200 for nuclear subs. The Polaris recruiting program is in its first year.

The Navy currently has three atomic submarines and two of the Polaris class. But several more are being built.

Its training program is timed to furnish crews as the craft are commissioned. Crewmen recruited directly from high schools will fill more than half the available billets.

Crews for the first nuclear submarines came from the regular Navy, mostly from conventional submarines. But regular Navy men have been slow to volunteer recently. The personnel bureau says there are several reasons.

3-YEAR COURSE

For one, it takes at least three years to train a man for a nuclear submarine job.

During that time he draws regular Navy pay. This hardly appeals to men on conventional subs who now get special, hazardous duty pay, and would be forced to give that up.

For another reason, training is a tough, around-the-clock, seven-day-a-week affair. Atomic submarines move around a great deal, and this means crews frequently are at sea for months at a time.

Liberty ports are few and far between. Many of the best foreign ports, and some in the U. S., aren't open to nuclear-powered craft.

NEW LOOK

(The Navy has asked the Defense Department to reinterpret regulations and authorize special pay during at least part of the nuclear training program.

It anticipates a favorable ruling, but the department has not yet acted.)

For a while, Navy tried ordering men to duty on nuclear submarines. This did not work out too well, either.

The teen-agers will be signed for six-year enlistments. (The average Navy enlistment is under four years.)

Many of the youngsters aren't old enough to commit themselves to that legally, but the Navy exacts or their parents to reenlist later.

LAND AND SEA

After boot camp, nuclear submarine crews take their training at New London, Conn. or Mare Island, Calif., later progressing to dry-land mock-up atomic ships at Arco, Ida., West Milton, N. Y. or Windsor Locks, Conn.

Sub Crews Get College Studies

CAMBRIDGE, Mass., Sept. 10 (AP).—Crew members of the Navy's Polaris missile-firing submarine, USS George Washington, can "go to college" when the atomic-powered submarine goes on operational patrol this fall.

They will have a chance to work for Harvard University credits—the first students to take a Harvard extension course away from the Boston area.

Through films of lectures telecast last spring by Boston's educational station WGBH-TV, the Polaris submarines will study the meaning of modern political revolutions to gain insight into their causes, development, and result.

The 15 kinescope-recorded lectures by Crane Brinton, McLean professor of ancient and modern history at Harvard, will be shown while the submarines are cruising underseas on patrol.

Assigned reading for the lectures will be available in the submarine's library.

When crewmen return to the United States submarine base at New London, Conn., the students will meet with Harvard teaching fellows for classroom instruction. Those who pass the final examination will receive one-quarter course credit (approximately two semester hours of college credit).

Crew members of other fleet ballistic missile submarines will have the same opportunity as other submarines become operational.

Judging by such news items, based upon official information, Navy Department concern with education is far from an academic matter. Admiral Rickover has contended that several of his speeches regarding education and national defense are in no way his official concern.

Introduction

THE NATIONAL DEFENSE EDUCATION ACT OF 1958 was passed by the Senate on August 22 and by the House on the following day, and was signed into Public Law 85–864 by President Eisenhower on September 2.

In passing the act, the Congress recognized that the defense and the security of the Nation are inseparably bound with education.

Foreword

While we can be proud of the great diversity and the strengths of our schools, the quality of education necessary to develop our human resources to meet the national needs and to satisfy the public interest can be provided only when our strengths are extended and our weaknesses are eliminated. The public's desire to accelerate the strengthening of educational programs was recognized by the Congress and reflected in the National Defense Education Act of 1958, which was signed into law by the President on September 2, 1958. The act authorizes expenditures of more than $1 billion over a 4-year period.

It is my privilege to present to the Congress, as provided by Section 1001(c) of Public Law 85–864, a report on our first year's stewardship, ending June 30, 1959.

LAWRENCE G. DERTHICK
United States Commissioner of Education

Extracts from a U. S. Government report on the National Defense Education Act authorizing expenditure of a billion dollars on the ground that "the defense and security of the Nation are inseparably bound with education". In justifying his copyrights Admiral Rickover has insisted, despite his own public statements to the contrary, that his speeches on education had nothing to do with his concerns as a high officer of the Navy Department and the Atomic Energy Commission. Moreover, he has disregarded the vast sums annually expended by the Defense Department, the Navy Department, and the Atomic Energy Commission on activities and projects involving the educational institutions. On March 6, 1959, for example, the Atomic Energy Commission awarded 440 research and development contracts to institutions of higher education.

"Today we must have schools which develop all . . . to the highest level of intellectual competence which they are capable; schools which help young people to understand the complex world of today and how it came to be what it is.

"My personal experience in developing nuclear power has convinced me that our schools do not produce enough qualified people to run our complex technological society. We have a chronic shortage of trained professionals which is not limited to scientists and engineers but is all-pervasive. Nor do we have enough broadly and liberally educated people with qualities of leadership to administer the work of trained professionals . . .

"Though I have never taken a course in 'education,' I have been running schools for years. Everyone in my atomic power group has taken a hand at some time or other at teaching what he has first had to teach himself about the new science of nuclear engineering. We have set up schools for our own engineers and for industry people, as well as for the officers and men who will operate our nuclear ships."

EDITORIAL VIEWS OF NEWSPAPERS ON COPYRIGHT
RESTRICTIONS BY PUBLIC OFFICIALS

"Can a public official copyright his speeches, granting the press the right to quote him only if and when he gives permission?

"A federal district judge in Washington, D. C. has just ruled to this effect. It is a ruling we consider in direct conflict with the First Amendment to the Constitution; we trust it will be reversed on appeal.

"The fact that Admiral Rickover appended the note, 'no permission needed for press use,' does not mitigate the danger inherent in this situation. The fact remains that the public, through its free press, was wranted access to Admiral Rickover's remarks only at the admiral's sufferance and not as a matter of right.

"It follows obviously that if a public official can copyright his public speeches he has at his disposal a weapon which can be used to thwart the people's right to know what their officials are doing and saying. This, we believe, is not in the public interest."—*San Jose Mercury*.

* * *

"The broad question of the public's right to know what a public official is thinking, writing and saying is left unanswered. . . .

"From this two questions arise: First . . . is the admiral implying that he has the right to give or withhold permission for use by newspapers or news periodicals? And second, if the courts should decide he has such a right on speeches or writing 'not a part of his official duties,' how broad or narrow a definition should the courts place on the term 'official duties?'

"When it comes to a public official, the public is entitled to know just about everything there is to know about him and there should be few things that should not be considered a part of his 'official' life. . . . If there is any hint of a public official's right to restrict the public's knowledge of him, then there should be a long, close look at the decision."—*Portland, Oregon Journal.*

* * *

"Vice Admiral Hyman Rickover has secured a Federal District Court ruling that he may copyright his speeches and that they may not be published without his permission. This is a strange ruling, and on the basis of available facts, it would seem to go to unreasonable lengths to protect the admiral.

"Any speech which any public official makes belongs to the public, and a vice admiral surely is a public official. Chances are the admiral wrote his speeches on government time, and the information he used in writing those speeches surely came because of his government service. . . . If he tries to get into the business of copyrighting speeches as he makes them, he's in mighty deep water even for an admiral.

"One of the main sidelines of generals and admirals now seems to be that of writing books about their experiences. The public helps enough in that writing now without having to see every word uttered by the admiral copyrighted for the admiral's own personal profit."—*Raleigh (N. C.) Times.*

* * *

"This nation esteems Admiral Rickover among its great men of modern electronic-nuclear science. We have benefited immeasurably by his genius. His tenacity of purpose in the fact of bureaucratic oversight and jealousy has been widely applauded. But the Admiral's claim that his public utterances should be private on the basis of commercial consideration is illogical.

"We cannot understand how any judge can determine that a man in public life who makes public statements may then copyright them and prevent reaching the public through normal news channels.

"In his public utterances he (Admiral Rickover) cannot disassociate himself from his position as an officer of the United States Navy, paid by the taxpayers. And he cannot consistently deny the right of the free press of America to report what he says."—*Honolulu Star-Bulletin.*

"If a nation expects to be ignorant and free,
in a state of civilization, it expects what
never was and never will be."

– Thomas Jefferson

Chapter 1

EDUCATION IS
OUR FIRST LINE OF DEFENSE
—MAKE IT STRONG

This book is a collection of speeches made during the last four years. Some have been shortened, others expanded, and some new material has been added to produce an orderly sequence.

Extracts from the preliminary pages of a compilation of speeches Admiral Rickover copyrighted early in 1959. The strictures against quotation are surprising in view of the fact that the book is composed of speeches issued as press releases by the Defense Department, Navy Department, and the Atomic Energy Commission. On October 20, 1960, the U. S. Court of Appeals ruled that most of the speeches had not been legally copyrighted. The Jefferson quote adds an ironic touch.

CONSTRAINT BY COPYRIGHT

"It would be alarming if Admiral Rickover or anyone else could, by copyrighting a public speech or a statement, prohibit or restrict the reporting of a speech or statement.

"We hope that no government official construes the opinion to mean that he can talk in public and, by a copyright, dictate how his speech is to be reported. That would be intolerable censorship."—*Des Moines Register.*

* * *

"The freedom of the press issue involved in Vice Admiral Hyman G. Rickover's effort to copyright his public speeches is yet to be finally resolved judicially.

"The trial court ruled that the speeches could be copyrighted, that even though they related to his official work they were not sufficiently a part of it to come within the public domain. That ruling (does) not settle the question of the press freedom to report and comment on public speeches subject to that copyright protection."—*Corpus Christi Caller.*

* * *

"A federal court ruling that Vice Admiral Hyman G. Rickover has the right to copyright his public speeches may make legal sense under the peculiar circumstances of the case, but we shudder slightly at what might conceivably flow from it.

"We certainly hope the salty admiral is not about to usher in an era when every public official will rush to the copyright office for protection of his right to exploit privately what he has learned in public service.

"The trend in view, at any rate, is not a healthy one from the standpoint of guaranteeing the broadest public access to public information."—*Buffalo News.*

* * *

"This is an unusual decision of far-reaching import, since the admiral is an employee of the United States government and the speeches of government officials have usually been looked upon as public property once they have been made available to the public.

"The Rickover case has numerous implications aside from his specialized knowledge of nuclear affairs, his own proclivity for speaking his mind and his desire to profit from work he may have performed while on government duty or during off-duty hours. One aspect of the case, however, that may come in for further scrutiny by the courts involves not his own time or talents but the time and talents of associates and subordinates.

"Rare is the government official of Rickover's rank, responsibilities and associations who does not make use of the literary abilities of others. The 'ghost writer' is a common necessity for many high placed men in

BRIEF FOR *AMICUS CURIAE*
SIGMA DELTA CHI,
PROFESSIONAL JOURNALISTIC FRATERNITY

IN THE

United States Court of Appeals

FOR THE DISTRICT OF COLUMBIA CIRCUIT

No. 15,463

PUBLIC AFFAIRS ASSOCIATES, INC., Trading as
PUBLIC AFFAIRS PRESS, *Appellant*

v.

VICE ADMIRAL HYMAN G. RICKOVER, *Appellee*

**Appeal from the United States District Court
for the District of Columbia**

HARRY N. ROSENFIELD
Attorney for Amicus Curiae
1735 De Sales Street, N.W.
Washington 6, D. C.

GRAY PRINTING, WASHINGTON, D. C.

Title page of the Sigma Delta Chi brief opposing the copy-right activities of Admiral Rickover. The oldest and largest professional organization in journalism, this society is composed of some 20,000 publishers, editors, and newsmen embracing all fields and all ranks of journalism. A prime purpose of Sigma Delta Chi is to fight encroachments on freedom of press. Opposition by Admiral Rickover's attorney prevented acceptance of the brief by the court.

A portion of the table of contents of the Sigma Delta Chi brief to the U. S. Court of Appeals. "On the facts of this case", the society stated, "it believes that the opinion [of Judge Holtzoff] is a serious curtailment of the Constitutional right of freedom of press under the First Amendment of the Constitution and of the right of the American people to freedom of information about the activities of their public officials". The U. S. Court of Appeals upheld Holtzoff in ruling that Rickover could have placed restrictions on his speeches if he had complied with copyright procedures.

public life. . . . Admiral Rickover may be unique in this respect. But there is little doubt that the activities of Washington 'ghosts' on the public pay rolls are closely allied with the legal and other issues in this case."—*Spokane Spokesman-Review.*

*   *   *

"Is everything that a public official does in his official capacity in the public domain? We think it ought to be.

"The Admiral's stipulation that newspapers may quote freely from his copyrighted speeches . . . does not settle the question his action has raised.

"A Government employe has no rights in an invention that he has developed as part of his official duties. This rule extends to devices which the employe develops on his own time but which are celarly related to his Government work. . . . If such regulations were extended to speeches of public officials Admiral Rickover would be unable to copyright speeches which he prepared and delivered as part of his official duties. . . .

"Should not the Government extend the sound principles of its patent rights to speeches and other material which can be copyrighted?"—*Washington Post.*

*   *   *

"Hitherto free American citizens have taken it for granted that speeches are in the public domain. Anybody can go and listen, and anybody can reproduce them in any way he chooses from a one-paragraph news account to a full text. . . . But all of a sudden Admiral Rickover contends that his speeches are for 'contemporaneous press use' only, which sounds as though they were in the public domain when uttered but thereafter mysteriously transformed themselves into the Admiral's private property. No wonder other Pentagon officials are forming in line to copyright their brain children.

"Clearly, if the Admiral were to write a novel, even say of life on an atomic sub, that would be his private property as much as any literary production written by any man. But what is in question here, speeches made by the Admiral as our boss atomic Admiral, look less like literary productions than part of his job. Often those speeches have been run off by Pentagon employes on government mimeograph machines, or have been printed and distributed by the government under the seal of the Department of Defense. What's private about that?

"Fortunately, this issue is going to be tested in court. The Public Affairs Press in Washington has filed a suit that should lead the courts to trace a proper borderline. There is a growing need for such a line."—*Hartford Courant.*

OPINIONS OF LEADING EDITORS

"I have never seen any justification for Admiral Rickover's copyrights. . . . I'd hate to see you drop your appeal of the Holtzoff decision. . . . His ruling sets up some bad possibilities and I certainly think it is important enough to go to a higher court."—*James S. Pope, Chairman of the Society of Information Committee of the American Society of Newspaper Editors and Executive Editor of the Louisville Courier-Journal.*

* * *

"I hope very much that you will keep up the cause. These things always have to be achieved by a small number of dedicated people, with the rest of those interested and the general public that benefits just going along for the ride."—*Herbert Brucker, Editor, Hartford Courant.*

* * *

"The case raises questions of interest to the press as a whole. . . . It is clear that the rest of us have everything to gain and nothing to lose in case you decide to test the issue to the fullest possible extent."—*Newbold Noyes, Jr., Executive Editor, Washington Evening Star.*

* * *

"Copyrighting by officials very definitely abridges the Constitutional principle of the free press in that it permits legal restriction on the press in discussing intelligently the people's business."—*V. M. Newton, Jr., Managing Editor, The Tampa Tribune.*

* * *

"The issues that your suit has raised, I completely agree, are of very great broad general importance. . . . The case undoubtedly does have disquieting implications."—*James Russell Wiggins, President of American Society of Newspaper Editors and Executive Editor of the Washington Post.*

* * *

"I am firmly convinced that the public utterances of any public official, relating to any aspect of public business, are not the property of the official, but of the public and should not be covered by copyright, or any other device to prevent or restrict their wide and free discussion. The reason was plainly stated by Thomas Jefferson: 'If a nation expects to be ignorant and free, in a state of civilization, it expects what never was and never will be.' "—*Gerald W. Johnson, Historian and Editorial Writer for Baltimore Sun.*

12

UNRESOLVED QUESTIONS

The Rickover case is important primarily because of the precedent it has set. This precedent has significant implications in that it involves the first known instance of a Federal official taking the position that his public speeches—speeches prepared, issued and disseminated as Government publications—are subject to copyright restrictions asserted by him in his private capacity and that by virtue of the licensing rights arising out of copyright ownership he can decide for himself who may quote him and under what circumstances.

What makes the Rickover case even more important is the fact that the recent decision of the Appeals Court [1] opens the door wide to more rather than less copyrighting by public officials. Although this court reversed the decision of the lower court and invalidated the copyrights of almost all of the 26 speeches at issue, it did so on the ground that the Admiral had not technically complied with the provisions of the Copyright Act. Despite all the official characteristics of the speeches and the Act's prohibition of copyrighting of official material, the court ruled they were private works the Admiral could have copyrighted had he duly observed the procedural requirements of the law.

The decision of the court establishes a particularly dangerous precedent in that it constitutes the first known judicial ruling to the effect that the seals and imprimaturs of government agencies can be used on works privately copyrightable (with or without indication of copyright) by officers of such agencies. Unwittingly, *this decision makes it impossible for the public or the press to determine when a statement by a government officer is official and therefore of considerable importance and when it is private and without any binding force.* If publications that appear to be official in every essential sense of that term are tolerated or sanctioned as private then, presumably, private publications appearing under official guise could be considered justifiable by persons seeking to misrepresent private matter as official.

Moreover, the Appeal Court decision is so broadly phrased that if the Supreme Court permits it to stand any and all public officials not specifically "commissioned . . . [by] the United States" to write for the

[1] U. S. Court of Appeals for the District of Columbia Circuit, October 20, 1960.

government can consider themselves free to copyright well nigh anything they write, regardless of what they write, the nature of the official information they use, and what facilities they employ in the preparation, processing, and dissemination of what they write. While the Appeals Court probably did not mean to sanction such copyrighting the fact remains that the door is now wide open to this practice.

In effect, the court ruled that although the duties of a public official are directly related, as in Admiral Rickover's case, to atomic energy and nuclear submarines, he can copyright his public statements on these very subjects because it is not his specified official duty to issue such statements.

Pointing out that the provision of the Copyright Act which prohibits copyrighting of government publications "creates a sea of troublesome questions", the Appeals Court enlarged this sea considerably by holding that only publications of the Government Printing Office "commissioned or printed at the cost and direction of the United States" are "authorized expositions on matters of governmental interests by governmental authority" that can be considered publications of the United States Government.

Moreover, the court does not take into consideration the fact that thousands of government publications are processed by and for governmental agencies through mimeograph, multilith, and other devices, often by private firms.

In ruling that copyrights cannot be placed on publications "commissioned at . . . direction of the United States" the court definitely contributed to clarification of the provision of the Copyright Act prohibiting copyright of government publications, but it erred by not taking into consideration the fact that *it is general practice for high public officials to commission themselves in connection with most of the things they do and say.* It is a matter of common knowledge that a high official rarely—if ever—feels inhibited about issuing a public statement because it had not been commissioned by someone other than himself. A vital reason for this is the fact that every official knows that although he is not specifically commissioned by the "United States" to deliver public pronouncements this is one of his fundamental responsibilities under our democratic form of government.

If a public officer is not "commissioned" to write for the federal government should he be completely free to consider as his personal property practically anything he may have occasion to write—regardless of the extent to which such material is prepared and processed with the benefit of official resources and facilities?

Rickover Loses Fight On Copyrighted Talks

By PHIL THOMAS
Star Staff Writer

Vice Admiral Hyman Rickover does not have a copyright on speeches he made between 1955 and 1958, the United States Court of Appeals ruled here today.

However, in the case of speeches after that date which Admiral Rickover marked copyright, the appellate court asked for further hearings.

In an opinion written by retired Supreme Court Justice Stanley Reed, sitting by designation on the appellate court, it was reasoned that since the content of the earlier speeches by the admiral were "open to the entire world . . . it is difficult to avoid the conclusion (that full distribution of the speeches constituted) their dedication to the public domain."

Question Remains

Justice Reed said there remains a question of whether or not he is entitled to a copyright on speeches issued after 1958—when the admiral put a notice on the speech copies.

The copyright notice gave permission for "contemporaneous press use," and Justice Reed sent back for further hearing in District Court the question of fair use of these later addresses "in compilations or in quotation or in criticism."

Judge John A. Danaher agreed with Justice Reed's opinion but Judge George T. Washington dissented, saying he felt the admiral did preserve "the exclusive right to publish the speeches in compiled form after their immediate news value passes away.

Justice Reed, in ruling as he did today, reversed the decision of a year ago by District Court Judge Alexander Holtzoff.

Copyright Challenged

Judge Holtzoff ruled against a suit brought by the Public Affairs Press of Washington, which sought to publish a compilation of the admiral's speeches, challenging a copyright the father of the atomic submarine claimed on the 23 speeches.

The publishing house claimed that the speeches were prepared by the admiral in his role as a Government official, and therefore were Government publications in the public domain.

The topics in the speeches included subjects from nuclear power to public education, and the texts were issued as press releases under Government letter heads.

Judge Holtzoff had held that literary products of a Government official that have some bearing on his work but not on his official duties, are not in the public domain.

Today's opinion agreed that "none of these papers is a governmental publication."

No Automatic Bar

"It cannot properly be said that a governmental official who speaks or writes of matter

This Washington Evening Star story of October 20, 1960 provided readers of that paper with an accurate account of the ruling of the U. S. Court of Appeals in regard to the Rickover copyrights. (Continued on next page).

with which he is concerned as an official is by the very fact of being such an official barred from copyright on his productions," Justice Reed said.

Agreeing with Judge Holtzoff on this point, Justice Reed said that if such statements are "called for by his official duties or (are) explanations as guides for official actions, they are barred from a copyright." However, the opinion added, this was not the case here.

But it pointed out that there was "no effort to limit distributions of the speeches delivered before December 1, 1958."

"Certainly when all of Admiral Rickover's acts of distribution are considered together," Justice Reed said, "it is difficult to avoid the conclusion that these acts, in their totality, constitute publication of the speeches and their dedication to the public domain."

"Very Grave Matter"

Disagreeing with Justice Reed's conclusions, Judge Washington said he felt "it is a very grave matter for a court to pronounce the forfeiture of an author's intellectual property.

"There is nothing in the law which would compel this court to deprive the creator of the right to reap financial benefits from these efforts because, at the time of their creation, they had the added virtue of being newsworthy events of immediate public concern," Judge Washington said.

Earlier Decision Is Modified

Court Upholds Rickover's Copyright

A high Government official or employe can protect his speeches and writings with a copyright as long as they are not related directly to his duties, the U. S. Court of Appeals ruled today.

The court, in a 2-1 decision written by retired Supreme Court Justice Stanley Reed, upheld the right of Vice Admiral Hyman G. Rickover to copyright speeches — as he has since December, 1958— as long as they are not Government publications or called for by his official duties.

But, it said, the Admiral lost the right of authorship of 20 speeches delivered on or before that date by distributing them so widely to the press and public and, consequently, putting them in the public domain.

"Any one was welcome to a copy," Justice Reed said.

The Court's ruling partially upset a decision of District Judge Alexander Holtzoff a year ago. Judge Holtzoff said Admiral Rickover can copyright speeches even if they have some bearing on his official duties.

He said then that restricted distribution of the Admiral's speeches does not mean abandonment of a property right or dedication to the public domain. Nor does it bar the author from later procuring a copyright when the speeches are published, Judge Holtzoff ruled.

In this respect the Appeals Court differed.

The law provides that no Government publication shall be copyrighted. Justice Reed said this refers to publications commissioned or printed at the cost and direction of the United States.

Admiral Rickover's speeches dealing with a wide variety of subjects, included chiefly education and nuclear power, were written on his own time. The court said "occasional use" of a Government secretary or multilithing machine for making copies would not mean they were being published at Government expense.

The case arose when Public Affairs Press, an educational publishing house, sought to use Admiral Rickover's speeches in a book. It asked the court to remove copyright restrictions.

3 Convicted

Eddie M. Harrison, 18, of 1212 Fourth-st nw, Orson G. White, 20, of 1631 Massachusetts-av se, and Joseph R. Sampson, 22, of 1915 Fourth-st nw, all colored, were found guilty yesterday of first-degree murder in the shotgun slaying, March 8, of gambler "Cider George" Brown, also colored.

Earlier Decision Is Modified

Rickover Loses Fight With Publisher

A high Government official or employe can protect his speeches and writings with a copyright as long as they are not related directly to his duties, the U. S. Court of Appeals ruled today.

The court, in a 2-1 decision written by retired Supreme Court Justice Stanley Reed, upheld the right of Vice Admiral Hyman G. Rickover to copyright speeches — as he has since December, 1958— as long as they are not Government publications or called for by his official duties.

But, it said, the Admiral lost the right of authorship of 20 speeches delivered on or before that date by distributing them so widely to the press and public and, consequently, putting them in the public domain.

"Any one was welcome to a copy," Justice Reed said.

The Court's ruling partially upset a decision of District Judge Alexander Holtzoff a year ago. Judge Holtzoff said Admiral Rickover can copyright speeches even if they have some bearing on his official duties.

He said then that restricted distribution of the Admiral's speeches does not mean abandonment of a property right or dedication to the public domain. Nor does it bar the author from later procuring a copyright when the speeches are published, Judge Holtzoff ruled.

In this respect the Appeals Court differed.

The law provides that no Government publication shall be copyrighted. Justice Reed said this refers to publications commissioned or printed at the cost and direction of the United States.

Admiral Rickover's speeches dealing with a wide variety of subjects, included chiefly education and nuclear power, were written on his own time. The court said "occasional use" of a Government secretary or multilithing machine for making copies would not mean they were being published at Government expense.

The case arose when Public Affairs Press, an educational publishing house, sought to use the pre-December, 1958 speeches in a book. It asked the court to remove copyright restrictions. The court said the speeches were not legally copyrighted.

Boy Blamed for Fires

An 11-year-old white boy who last night came up with a hose to put out a small fire he later admitted starting at Carroll and Laurel avenues, Takoma Park, has confessed starting two other fires — one of which he stayed to watch — in the 7000 block of Carroll av, police said.

"You pays yer nickle and you takes yer choice." The story in center appeared in first edition of the Washington Daily News on October 20, 1960. The story at the bottom appeared in a later edition of the same paper. Only important difference between the stories in the underlined last sentence of bottom item.

In effect and in fact every public servant above the middle clerical grades is commissioned to write for the government. If this were not the case modern government would be inchoate. It is difficult to imagine a government transacting its affairs wholly via memory, face to face conversations, and telephone communication. Without written presentation of research, recommendation, and decision, government would be well nigh impossible and government publications merely rhetorical gibberish.[1]

It is just because most public servants could not possibly fulfill their responsibilities without extensive writing that ability to express oneself satisfactorily by this process is a *sine qua non* of employment by government. And it is because authoritativeness rather than literary skill are primary considerations in all governmental writing that most of it is necessarily done by expert specialists—by economists, political scientists, physicists, etc.—rather than by writers as such.

With good reason, government has in recent years increasingly relied upon editors for assistance in polishing and revising the writings of expert specialists. Significantly, most of the countless writings published by the Government Printing Office are credited to expert specialists—to geologists, statisticians, physicists, etc.—and not to writers.

And it is with good and sufficient reasons that acts and statements by officials are generally considered privileged by the courts. Without immunity from personal liability while fulfilling their responsibilities government officers could not effectively carry out the nation's laws.

The duties of an inspector for the Food and Drug Administration may differ substantially from those of the head of this agency, but both necessarily enjoy discretionary powers consonant with their responsibilities. But for such powers neither could cope with the variables and unpredictables that confront them every day.

If a public officer, high or low, acting unmistakably in his official capacity does or says something directly related to his duties, it would seem reasonable, indeed unavoidable, to assume that what he said or did is official and therefore privileged. If, moreover, what is said or done is not specifically outlined in his duties but is directly related to them by official custom and practice then what is said or done is for all practical purposes official in every essential sense of that term.[2]

Let a public officer be sued for anything said or done that relates to his official capacity and he does not hesitate a moment to claim official privilege. And, by and large, the courts will give him the benefit of any reason-

---

[1] In the course of a "Meet the Press" broadcast on January 24, 1960, Admiral Rickover stated that about "75%" of his time was occupied by writing of various sorts. Whether any of this time was devoted to writing what he copyrights he did not disclose.

DEPARTMENT OF THE NAVY
OFFICE OF THE SECRETARY
WASHINGTON 25, D. C.

2 3 JUN 1960

Dear Mr. Schnapper:

This will reply to your letter of 13 June 1960 requesting
information pertaining to Miss Theresa Leone's service in
the Department of the Navy, particularly with respect to
the circumstances attendant the preparation of copies of
speeches copyrighted by Admiral Rickover.

The information requested by you appears to bear upon a
matter in litigation between Public Affairs Associates,
Incorporated, and Admiral Rickover, and now pending before
the U. S. Court of Appeals. It is the practice of the
Department of the Navy to decline to furnish, at the
request of the parties litigant, official records or
copies thereof or other information, to be used in the
course of the proceedings, or to grant permission to
such parties or their attorneys to make preliminary or
informal examination of the records. However, the
Department of the Navy will promptly furnish copies of
official records or other information in such cases upon
call of the court before which the litigation is pending.

Your request for information pertaining to this litigated
matter is therefore declined.

Sincerely yours,

W. B. Franke

Public Affairs Press
419 New Jersey Avenue, S. E.
Washington 3, D. C.

Attention Mr. M. B. Schnapper, Executive Director

The difficulty of ascertaining the simplest of facts is reflected by this
letter from Secretary of the Navy W. B. Franke. All that had been
requested of the Secretary was information as to whether Miss Leone
was an employee of the Navy at the time of Admiral Rickover's
copyrights. Note that Secretary Franke took the position that no
data whatsoever about the status of Navy employees could be furnished unless court orders were secured. Inasmuch as such orders
would involve additional legal proceedings Public Affairs Press was
not able to ascertain officially that Miss Leone was a Navy employee.
The reader can well imagine the expense and trouble involved in
securing the mass of information in the present report.

able doubt if there is more than a modicum of official justification for what he said or did.

From the viewpoint of the American people it would be unfortunate indeed if government officials did not enjoy privileged status, discretionary powers, and discretionary powers. But it would also be highly unfortunate if public officials could switch from official privilege to private privilege at will or at whim.

[2] "Governmental activities do not allow differentiation between what is private and what is public," in the opinion of Judge Leon Yankwich of the U.S. District Court. "All the business which persons in public office, high or low, perform is of a public nature. So there is no conflict, as in the case of privacy, between individual rights and the public's demands—but rather between the right of the public to be informed and the arrogative right of persons in public office to withhold the information." (The Administration of Justice and the Right to Know, p. 5).

In refusing to hold an attorney guilty of contempt of court because he had told newspapermen about statements made by a public officer, the Supreme Court of California held that "it is a first principle that the people have the right to . . . the greatest publicity to the acts of those holding positions of public trust, and the greatest freedom . . . that, consistent with truth and decency, are regarded as essential to the public welfare." [2] (In re Shortridge, 1893, 99 Cal. 526, 530.)

13

ADDENDA

It is relatively easy for anyone to obtain a copyright. It is difficult and very costly to render a copyright invalid. Result: a situation distinctly convenient for persons not inhibited about taking advantage of a weak law.

It is easy to obtain a copyright because the only basic requirement is that the claimant assert he is the owner. No proof of ownership need be furnished; if legitimacy is lacking, a little gall, possibly mixed with a touch of illusion or presumption, will go a long way.

Moreover, a person abusing the copyright law can easily hide himself from public view. He doesn't have to represent himself as author (which he may not be and which isn't even necessary as a pretense). If he is the author and doesn't want to disclose this he can adopt a convenient pseudonym. Or he can — as author, as author-pretender, or as proprietor-pretender—arrange for copyrighting through an agent or "front".

A copyright claimant doesn't even have to go to the expense of printing what he seeks to copyright. Under the present statutes a copyright can be obtained simply by "processing" (typing, multilithing or mimeographing will do) and depositing with the Library of Congress only two copies of the work for which copyright is desired. True several more copies should be around for the sake of the record, but this hardly works a hardship on a claimant intent upon obtaining the benefits of copyright without accepting any disadvantages. While the copyright registration asks the claimant to state when he made his work "public", it is not incumbent upon him to substantiate this in any way. Indeed he does not even have to pretend that he has made one copy of the work available for more than a minute to anyone but himself.

These are hardly circumstances beneficial from the public's viewpoint.

In approving the copyright restrictions Admiral Rickover had placed on 26 speeches relating to his governmental work and the responsibilities of the agencies of which he is one of the highest officials, Judge Alexander Holtzoff of the U.S. District Court ruled that the Admiral had not been specifically hired to write or deliver speeches. To the learned and highly esteemed Judge this seemed to be ample justification of the Admiral's copyrights and sufficient reason to disregard or minimize all other factors.

There can be no question that Judge Holtzoff's decision was swayed by no other considerations but justice as he saw it. However, justice as he saw it must have been influenced by the fact that in the course of his official duties as Special Assistant to the Attorney General from 1924 to 1945 and as Judge of the U.S. District Court for the District of Columbia since 1945 he had himself been party to publication, under private and exclusive arrangements, of writings of his own relating to his official duties.

Among the dozen works credited to Judge Holtzoff in the catalog cards of the Library of Congress are the following:

"Federal Procedural Forms For Use in Civil and Criminal Actions", 1940.

"New Federal Procedure and the Courts", 1940.

"Practice Under Federal Rules of Procedure", 1940.

"Handling of Tort Claims Against the Federal Government", 1942.

"Federal Rules of Criminal Procedure, With Notes Prepared Under the Direction of the Advisory Committee Appointed by U.S. Supreme Court", 1946.

"Federal Practice and Procedure, With Forms: Civil and Criminal", 1950-51.

It must be presumed that the arrangements Judge Holtzoff entered into in this connection were perfectly proper and that nothing the least questionable was involved. To all indications none of these publications was of a predominantly official character. However, it is difficult to presume that he was in no way subconsciously swayed by the fact that his approval of Admiral Rickover's private publication arrangements constituted approval of his own acts along different but somewhat similar lines.

For the free-wheeling public official and the publishing house that has the benefit of his "private" cooperation there are few problems. Under present conditions it appears to be extraordinarily easy for an official to decide that material prepared (or preparable) by or for him or his agency is of a private nature and therefore copyrightable. This situation is, of course, highly advantageous for publishers who are in a position to pay large sums for exclusive rights to "inside information" about governmental affairs (such articles usually pay off in that they help boost circulation as well as advertising revenues) or for "scoop" books with best seller or captive sales possibilities.

In one of the earliest criticisms of the monopolistic nature of copyrighting, Lord Camden called attention to the fact that its abuse could permit a small number of publishers to hold tight reins on printed knowledge. "All our learning," he warned Parliament in the 1770's, "will be locked up in the hands of the Tonsons and the Lintons of the age, who will set what price upon it their avarice chooses to demand, till the public become as much their slaves as their own hackney compilers are."

Applied to present-day circumstances Lord Camden's words are a timely warning. Aided and abetted by high government officials, several of the nation's largest publishing houses today hold, for example, exclusive rights to works containing the knowledge amassed by the United States government, at enormous expense to the American people, in atomic energy and cognate fields.

In view of all the copyrighting that public officials are doing these days and recent Congressional approval of a measure making the government liable for infringement of copyrights, it is only a matter of time before public officials will start suing the government for copying material which these very officials obtained from the government. And it will come as no great surprise when it is found that copyrighting officials somehow appeared to have encouraged the violations for which damages are claimed.

Historically, it has long been the custom for public officials to facilitate fulfillment of their responsibilities through public speeches. Some of the most important policies and plans of the national government have first been presented to the American people through speeches by their officials. On lower levels of government, speech making has not been quantitatively neglected; such neglect as has existed has been purely qualitative.

In 1933 the banking panic was allayed when President Roosevelt took to the radio to announce temporary closing of all banks and to reassure the people about the long-term safety of their money.

The fireside chats of FDR in the 1930's were the beginning of a custom of reporting to the people that has become indispensible to the men who have succeeded him in the White House. A direct outgrowth of this custom is the recent tendency of Cabinet members to report to the American

---

"Copyright admits of philosophic thinking more than most other parts of the law. Yet the philosophy of the subject has been somewhat submerged in the statutes and case-law because of the pressure of practical problems of narrow scope which demanded immediate solution. Fortunately, in surveying the principles of copyright reform we can get help from outsiders. Probably no branch of the law has received so much valuable comment from laymen." *Zechariah Chafee, Jr.* in "Reflections on the Law of Copyright," *Columbia Law Review*, July, 1945.

THE TRUMAN PROGRAM

Addresses and Messages by President Harry S. Truman

INTRODUCTION BY
SENATOR FRANCIS J. MYERS

EDITED BY M. B. SCHNAPPER

The copyright notice in this case pertained only to book creativity. In the case of compilations of speeches by public officials such as Vice President Nixon, Senator Kennedy, Admiral Rickover, and others it's general practice to insert the following type of notice on the copyright page: "No part of the book may be reproduced in any form without permission in writing from the publisher, except by reviewer wishing to quote brief passages in connection with a review written for inclusion in a magazine, or newspaper or broadcast".

151

TEXT OF OFFICIAL REPORT AND RELATED DOCUMENTS

War and Postwar Adjustment Policies

BY BERNARD M. BARUCH AND JOHN M. HANCOCK

American Council on Public Affairs
WASHINGTON, D. C.

Cover of a book published by the predecessor of Public Affairs Press. Adjoining its copyright notice—designed to protect features devised by the publisher—is the following statement: "Any portion of this volume may be quoted or reprinted. Due credit should, of course, be given to the authors and the publisher".

people via speeches before and after participation in meetings with the heads of other nations.

In 1947 America's allies throughout the world were greatly heartened when Secretary of State George C. Marshall announced from a rostrum at Harvard University his now famous Marshall Plan providing economic aid for economically distressed nations.

Those who insist that copyright law is rooted in the doctrines of private property rather than advancement of the public interest contend that the copyright owner is wholly within his rights if he chooses not to make available to the public that which belongs to him.

Regarding the private property concept, Thomas O. Baker states: [1]

"Advocates of the property concept propose that literary works are things which can be owned and possessed and that statutes are merely means of protecting the property interests of the owners. This property takes on two characteritstics: It is corporeal property in the sense that the author has a property right in the manuscript as much as he might have a right in any other tanglible personal property. Further, there is an incorporeal property carrying a power to determine whether the work shall be published at all, the manner in which, if published, it shall be done, and to whom." [2]

In dealing with the hybrid characteristics of copyright property, Justice Holmes stated:

"The notion of property starts, I suppose, from confirmed possession of a tangible object and consists in the right . . . [of] doing with it as one wills. But in copyright property . . . [the] right to exclude . . . restrains the sponaneity of men where but for it there would be nothing of any kind to hinder their doing as they saw fit." [3]

In pointing up the problems that have arisen because present-day interpretations of copyright law do not take into adequate consideration the fundamental reasons for the law, Dr. Luther Evans stated trenchantly in a treatise he wrote in his capacity as head of the Library of Congress and administrator of the Copyright Office:

"The diversity of juristic concepts as to the true basis of copyright has impressed many students of the subject. This has complicated efforts at agreement on definition and statements of principle not only in the inter-

[1] "The Property Concepts of Copyright Law", Thomas O. Baker, Missouri Law Review, Vol. 22, 1957, p. 202.

[2] The Protection and Marketing of Literary Property, Philip Wittenberg, 1937, p. 11.

[3] White-Smith Music Publishing Co. v. Apollo Co., 209, U.S. 1, 1908.

CONSTRAINT BY COPYRIGHT

national field but has also retarded the solution of pressing practical problems of detail in the domestic law of various countries. Adherents to the view that the right of an author to control, even after publication, the copying or reproduction in any form of the creation of his intellect is a property right essentially identical to that in a physical object moulded by an artisan with his hands or to a crop taken by a farmer from his soil, find it difficult to reconcile themselves to the thinking of those who assert copyright to be a privilege granted by the state for a limited duration in the public interest. Others deny the validity of either of these views and contend that copyright can only be adequately understood as in essence the extension of the creator's personality; that is, as an application of the doctrine of the right of privacy. On other occasions copyright has been spoken of as one of those natural rights more popular in a day of earlier political debate of which we may today be witnessing a revival as we hammer out codes of human and civil rights for universal acceptance."[4]

In discussing the importance of the Bill of Rights, Chief Justice Charles Evans Hughes called particular attention to the fact that James Madison felt the courts would best be able to safeguard the provisions of the Bill if they became Constitutional amendments. In his book, "The Supreme Court of the United States", Justice Hughes commends to the reader the following words by Madison:

"If they are incorporated into the Constitution, independent tribunals of justice will consider themselves in a peculiar manner the guardians of those rights; they will be an impenetrable bulwark against every assumption of power in the Legislative or Executive; they will be naturally led to resist every encroachment upon rights expressly stipulated for in the Constitution by the declaration of rights."

[4] "Copyright and Public Interest." Bulletin of the New York Public Library 1949, p. 200.

154